THERAPIST DISCLOSURE

The Use of Self
in Psychotherapy

THERAPIST DISCLOSURE

The Use of Self
in Psychotherapy

Myron F. Weiner, M.D.
Clinical Associate Professor of Psychiatry,
University of Texas Health Science
Center at Dallas

BUTTERWORTHS

Boston   London

The Butterworth Group

United States
Butterworth (Publishers) Inc.
19 Cummings Park
Woburn, MA 01801

England
Butterworth & Co. (Publishers) Ltd.
88 Kingsway
London WC2B 6AB

Australia
Butterworth Pty Ltd.
586 Pacific Highway
Chatswood, NSW 2067

Canada
Butterworth & Co. (Canada) Ltd.
2265 Midland Avenue
Scarborough, Ontario M1P 4S1

New Zealand
Butterworths of New Zealand Ltd.
26–28 Waring Taylor Street
Wellington 1

South Africa
Butterworth & Co. (South Africa)
 (Pty) Ltd.
152–154 Gale Street, Durban

Printed in the United States of America.

Cataloging in Publication Data
Library of Congress Cataloging in Publication Data

Weiner, Myron F.
  Therapist disclosure.

  Bibliography: p.
  Includes index.
  1. Psychotherapist and patient. 2. Psychotherapy.
3. Self-disclosure. I. Title. [DNLM: 1. Psycho-
therapy—Methods. 2. Psychotherapy, Group—Methods.
WM420 W429t}
RC480.8.W44   616.8'914   77-25491
ISBN 0-409-95070-X

To those who have been so much a part of me—
Eve, Jack, Dan, Gary, and Jan

Contents

Preface

The original impetus for this book was a troublesome interaction with a patient that contributed significantly to a therapeutic impasse. I was unable to resolve the impasse, and the patient sought further treatment with another therapist. It was tempting to blame the patient for being unmotivated and uncooperative. Instead, I set out to search for those elements in the patient, myself, and our relationship that acted as stumbling blocks. In retrospect, one element stood out sharply: my attempt, by being personally open, to facilitate the patient's sharing with me. It would have been easy enough to decide never again to be personally open with a patient. On the other hand, I was aware that while I wanted to be myself with some patients, I had no difficulty remaining neutral and undisclosed with others. I decided to find out what made the difference so that I might conduct psychotherapy on a rational basis and yet have the freedom to be myself when it was not detrimental to my patients. And I also set out to discover if being one's self is ever a positive element in the therapeutic relationship.

This book is the result of my investigation, which has lasted almost nine years. The original nucleus of this work was presented at the annual meeting of the Golden Gate Group Psychotherapy Society in 1969, under the title, "Nudity Versus Neutrality in Group Psychotherapy." As I had hoped, the title drew a large audience. After the audience recovered from its disappointment that we were not dealing with physical undress, we had a lively discussion. Other lively discussions followed in various professional arenas, including the annual meeting of the American Group Psychotherapy Association, conferences in the Department of Psychiatry at the University of Texas Health Science Center at Dallas, and at Timberlawn Foundation in Dallas.

I have had the opportunity to publish related material and work out my ideas in the *American Journal of Psychotherapy, Group Process, Diseases of the Nervous System, Psychosomatics*, the *American Journal of Psychiatry*, and *Adolescent Psychiatry*. Attempting to unite my ideas and observations in a single work has contributed significantly to their further evolution. I could not have fully grasped the significance of much of the material I had developed for different patient populations and different therapeutic circumstances had I not attempted to tie it all together. The material on countertransference was formulated at the conclusion of my other observations. At that point, the ideas were inescapable.

I am grateful for the patience and support of the people who have worked with me over the years of preparation and growth of this work. Dr. Alvin North made a detailed critique of an early draft. Drs. Robert Herbert and Jean Roberts shared their reactions to a later draft, as did Dr. Henry Grunebaum. My son, Gary Weiner, helped clarify my style and correct my grammar. Dr. Jerry Lewis asked pertinent questions and gave needed encouragement.

Many people who attended my presentations asked penetrating, stimulating questions that spurred my investigations. My family has shown genuine interest in the mountain of papers that has accumulated over the years, as it moved from living room to dining room to study, depending on my mood and the place in which inspiration struck me. The burden of typing has been cheerfully borne for the last five years by my secretary, Margaret Williams Fitch, who has managed to keep smiling in the face of endless revisions.

Myron F. Weiner, M.D.
April 1, 1977

THERAPIST DISCLOSURE

The Use of Self
in Psychotherapy

1.

Introduction

This book is divided into two sections. In part one, "General Considerations," I define being one's self, propose a classification of self-disclosure, examine self-disclosure in a historical context, review the research literature, and place self-disclosure by the therapist into the general framework of psychotherapeutic interventions. In part two, I attempt to sort out the indications and the contraindications to being one's self with patients, using the material presented in part one as my frame of reference. While this approach is useful for clarity, it is also a bit repetitious. I have, to a degree, sacrificed conciseness for clarity.

Because of the special demands placed on the therapist and the therapeutic relationship by adolescents and borderline patients, I have included more specific details on psychosexual development, psychopathology, therapeutic goals, and therapeutic strategy for these two groups than for other age groups and diagnostic categories.

The material on group therapy is dealt with separately because the therapeutic mechanisms of individual therapy are often widely divergent from the therapeutic mechanisms used in group therapy and because the treatment process in groups is greatly complicated by the use of cotherapists, a strategy now widely accepted in clinical practice and nearly universal in training centers.

Because of the ubiquity of countertransference in ongoing psychotherapies and the ease with which it can be rationalized or acted upon to the detriment of patient and therapist, it became evident that the relationship between countertransference and self-disclosure warranted special consideration.

Most of the clinical examples are derived from my own practice. I have tried to include sufficient information about the patient and the therapeutic relationship to make the material understandable, but I have omitted data that might identify the patient. I have included material on disclosures that were helpful, harmful, and irrelevant. I based my judgment on their impact on the patient's subsequent clinical course, being aware that a clinical example is only of value if its consequences are carefully followed over an extended period of time.

I use the terms *self-disclosure, use of self, being one's self, being real*, and *openness* to designate portions of the process of being one's self with patients. These terms do not imply that the therapist abandons his role as therapist. They refer to a type of therapy that takes into account the therapist as a fellow human being in relation to his patient: a situation in which the therapist offers more to a patient than professional expertise, but not his entire self. Being one's self acknowledges that, like the patient, the therapist has a history and a personality, both of which are relevant variables in the therapeutic process. Because this is a clinical rather than a philosophical work, I define "self" operationally, in terms of the various ways in which a person can be known. One's self, at an intrapsychic level, is that which one can experience of one's self at a given point in time. At an interpersonal level, it is that which is experienced by the individuals in one's interpersonal field at any given moment. One's entire self is never completely visible or available. And one's self is never entirely the same from moment to moment.

In attempting to be myself with patients, I often find I'm not the person I think I am or that I'm sharing myself for reasons other than those I tell myself. Even when patients see me as I see myself, it doesn't always have the effect I anticipate. While many patients profit from an existential encounter, many do not. In fact, some are hurt. As I become more self-aware, I become more conscious of my tendencies to self-disclose to gratify transference expectations, to act out my countertransference, and to indulge in narcissistic self-display. I have concluded that one cannot naively be one's self with patients, in spite of the Rogerian notion that genuineness, unconditional positive regard, and accurate empathy are the *sine qua non* of successful psychotherapy. There is no substitute for mature self-awareness combined with technical expertise to ensure that one's intrusion as a person into the lives of patients will be for the sake of furthering the patients' emotional growth. And, there is no substitute (including empathic awareness, which is often the therapist's projection onto the patient) for adequate knowledge of the patient's psychological makeup, the quality of his interaction with the therapist, and the reality situation in which patient and therapist function during the therapy session and in their lives outside the therapeutic hour.

I do not advocate the use of self-disclosure by all mental health professionals. I advocate only its reasoned use by those who choose to employ it. My intent is to share my experiences and my perception of the scientific literature in the hope of creating an objective climate in an area where emotionalism holds sway even among the most sophisticated professionals. I find self-disclosure to be more useful with certain groups of patients and in certain therapeutic situations. With most patients, therapeutic neutrality is generally more useful than revealing myself as a person.

In this respect, I differ from the existentialist who claims that the central problem of humankind is alienation and that to continue in the psychotherapeutic process to view one's fellow man as an object perpetuates his core problem. Some objectification of the patient is necessary to enable one to take a history, do an examination, and on that basis, formulate an initial therapeutic approach. Most patients do not seek an existential encounter as part of therapy. They are more concerned with relief of symptoms. It is only when patient and therapist alike find they must deal with one another as individual personalities to make the treatment work that such an encounter becomes valid. Otherwise, it is only a gratuitous personal and philosophical interest of the therapist that may obstruct the course of treatment for the patient, who merely wants to get about his business.

What are the basic issues related to the therapist's use of himself as a person in psychotherapy? In my own practice, the issue of whether or not to interject myself as a person arises almost every day. At times, I am pressured by my patients to be more open. At other times, the pressure arises within me. Under both circumstances, I ask myself whether or not to disclose, to what degree, and what aspect of myself will be the most advantageous to disclose. I then ask myself the significance of each decision I make, whether it is to disclose or to be neutral. I wonder about the role of honesty in the therapeutic relationship. My instincts often urge me to be honest. But honest about what? My diagnosis? My feelings about the patient? Is there a point at which my honesty will facilitate the patient's growth and another point at which certain kinds of honesty will be detrimental to my patient and to me?

Psychoanalysis holds that the therapist should assume a basically neutral stance and be known to the patient primarily in terms of his professional role. In this way, the transference is not obscured and the therapist refrains from acting on his countertransference feelings, which further complicate the therapeutic process. I agree with this premise. A professional relationship differs from social relationships in that a clear contract is established to perform a service for monetary compensation. The contract calls for (in Buber's terms) an I-it relationship. Are patient and therapist handicapped by such a contract? By accepting such a contract, does the therapist rule himself as a person out of the therapeutic process, thereby ensuring still another loss of a potential I-thou relationship and a continuing experience of partial dehumanization for the patient?

Existential psychotherapists are concerned with premature closure: that is, looking at a person as a diagnosis rather than as a person whom one diagnoses temporarily while getting better acquainted with him as a person. The existentialists call the avoidance of premature closure the process of "keeping looking"—a willingness to reformulate one's evaluation of the patient and one's relationship to him on the basis of continually unfolding evidence, rather than basing one's therapeutic efforts on the initial formal evaluation and then shutting one's mind to all subsequent data. The same applies to the therapist. He must continually "keep looking" at himself in the therapeutic relationship to understand at what point he is tempted to be open, at what point he feels defensive, and at what other point he is comfortably neutral.

Obviously, the psychotherapist is always exposed to some degree to his patient. It is the therapist's responsibility to ascertain the ways in which he is exposed and to determine the impact of these exposures on the therapeutic process. He may then attempt to regulate the type and degree of disclosures he makes, or he may simply note the impact of his person on the patient and watch for fluctuations as signs of changes in the patient-therapist relationship or in the patient's intrapsychic life.

One can avoid the difficulties of self-observation and decision making by deciding to be either open or nondisclosing to all patients. Such a step will certainly simplify the life of the therapist. It may, however, do considerable violence to the human needs of the patient.

I also wish to raise the question of the use of one's self to manipulate the patient's feelings. Under some circumstances, self-disclosure by the therapist can serve as inauthentic gimmickry by which the therapist discloses or exaggerates some aspect of his personality to elicit certain feelings or encourage certain reactions. The therapist may be "rough" to help mobilize a patient's aggression. He may be kind to provide a corrective emotional experience. Patients who are manipulated in this way may have difficulty knowing when to believe the therapist. The patient rightly wants to know when he is being put on and when the therapist genuinely feels what he says. When used to manipulate, the "openness" that one would normally expect to decrease the personal distance beween therapist and patient tends to reinforce the subject-object, I-it aspect of the relationship and the patient's view of himself as an object to be manipulated by others. Accordingly, one would expect that manipulative self-disclosures are probably most useful in short-term therapeutic contacts and least useful in psychotherapeutic treatment in which exploration of the therapist-patient relationship (transference-countertransference) is the primary therapeutic vehicle.

The greatest therapeutic possibility for openness with patients lies in its informational value. The patient is able to obtain information about the person with whom he is dealing; thus, he is able to clarify the real relationship between the therapist and himself, to become aware of the transference distortions, and to obtain real information about the world in which he lives and his impact upon it, as directly experienced by the therapist. This type of interpersonal feedback is the most highly valued aspect of group psychotherapy: one person openly acknowledging the impact of another upon himself for the purpose of supplying a clear view of the other's interpersonal operations.

Another possible, but more controversial, effect of therapist disclosure is partial identification of the patient with the therapist. Many family and group therapists implicitly and explicitly offer themselves as models of healthy behavior. Traditionally, the role of identification in the curative process has been played down or has been derogated as too closely resembling suggestion, a device used by charismatic healers, but not by "legitimate" professionals, for whom some form of insight is the only acceptable therapeutic medium. Identification and suggestion are decried as superficial means; only insight achieves lasting change.

With the rise of more directive therapies addressed to the alleviation of specific symptoms rather than to revision of the personality as a whole, and based on substantial evidence from social psychology, therapists who operate as teams now offer their relationship with their cotherapists as a paradigm of healthy relatedness. The usefulness of identification by the patient is of course limited by the personalities of the therapists, the appropriateness of such an identification for the patient, and the patient's capacity to identify positively with some healthy aspect of another person.

I deal only briefly with the issue of sexual intimacy between therapist and patient. There are a number of reasons for not making a more extensive presentation. The development of sexual intimacy between therapist and patient, regardless of the initiator, is a clear exploitation of the therapeutic relationship for another form of gratification. A therapist's choice when faced with a sexual approach by his patient is a clear one: to be a healer or a prostitute. He is certainly free to choose the latter but not to dignify it by calling it "therapy." The patient who is sexually approached by his therapist must choose between alleviating his emotional problem and gratifying the therapist's and his own sexual needs. Again, he is free to choose the latter but must accept the responsibility for diverting his attention from resolving his emotional problems to gratifying the therapist's and, presumably, his own sexual needs.

Some individuals view therapy as a transitional relationship. One rehearses in the therapeutic hour for dealing with situations in the outside world. Surely, it can be argued, sexual behavior between therapist and patient can serve as a bridge to a more satisfying sexual life outside of therapy. Although this logic works well for many kinds of behavior, sexual behavior is an important exception to the rule. Once sexually involved, therapist and patient have enormous difficulty getting unstuck and, in the process, frequently damage one another or damage the possibility of further emotional growth for both.

As a psychotherapist, I make certain assumptions: there is unconscious mental activity in the form of active, unconscious resistance by the patient's ego to accepting unconscious material (for example, by repression or projection) and resistance to awareness of the ego defense mechanisms involved. Additionally, there are interpersonal resistances based on transference and abetted by the therapist's own transference reactions. Finally, patient and therapist alike will attempt to act on, rather than become aware of, the unconscious material stimulated by the therapeutic process. It is the therapist's greater self-awareness that keeps the process of therapy on course. His expertise, his active participation, and the motivation of the patient for relief of suffering provide the driving forces.

Part One
General Considerations

2.

Historical Perspectives

Philosophical Underpinnings

A historical view of the therapist's use of himself as a person must take into account the values of scientific thinkers and researchers. Certain value systems encourage a view of the patient as object; others, as a focus of involvement. At the time of Freud's first published observations on hysteria in 1893, a fundamental premise of the sciences was that man and nature could be objectified and that the best means for discovering the truth about nature was detached observation. From the time of Copernicus, science had accepted the possibility of the neutral, uninvolved observer who, following the method of Descartes, could begin to distinguish the essence of natural phenomena from their surface appearance.[1] The view that essence could be distinguished from matter originated with Plato and was reinforced by Hegel many centuries later.[2] In the mid-nineteenth century, Kierkegaard held that man participates, even in cognition, with all his being—temporal, spatial, historical, psychological, sociological, and biological. This does not deny the possibility of detached, quantitative measurement; it emphasizes that one must participate in a self to know what it is, but by participating, the self is changed, and both subject and object are transformed by the act of knowing.[3] Later, existentialists (Rollo May in psychology and Ludwig Binswanger in psychiatry) ascribed to the post-Renaissance subject-object cleavage of Western thought an essential part of modern man's psychological problems—alienation from himself and others through objectification.[4]

Harry Stack Sullivan, adopting the point of view of social psychology, went so far as to define psychiatry as the study of interpersonal relations and to conclude that the data of psychiatry arise only in participant observation. He held that one cannot become aware of what another person does without becoming personally involved. One's principal instrument of observation is one's self, and the processes and changes in process that make up one's data occur not in subject person or object person, but in the situation created between them.[5]

Continuing along the same path, May postulated that the despair and lack of meaningful sense of being engendered by modern man's alienation can only be relieved in the context of a real relationship, not by introspection or dispassionate study by a neutral observer.[6]

The theoretical underpinnings of the issue of the therapist's use of himself lies, then, in the antithesis of the detached therapeutic observer and the idea that, when two people encounter each other in a cooperative effort, they begin a process that is the resultant vector of forces originating in both. This divergence of viewpoints among psychotherapists, while in existence for many years previously, surfaced vigorously with the advent of the so-called third force in psychology—the humanistic psychology movement. Carl Rogers was one of the early leaders of this movement, which essentially agreed with the existential position, but Rogers' stand was based on research data from psychotherapy rather than a system of philosophical values.[7, 8] Rogers' view was pragmatic rather than philosophical, and with his work we depart from the broad issue of detachment versus involvement to concrete issues of psychotherapeutic technique.

Use of Self as Technique

Currently, there is greater emphasis on the use of self-disclosure as a therapeutic technique. The controversy over self-exposure has polarized about a continuum from the "nude" position to the "neutral" position. The epitome of neutrality is the fabled analytic "blank screen," or the reflective Rogerian client-centered therapist. The analytic neutral therapist holds that he is a blank screen onto which the patient can project and subsequently work through his formerly unconscious fantasies. He claims to minimize transference gratification and to be able to refrain from acting out his countertransference. The Rogerian "mirror" advocate (Carl Rogers has himself departed from this position) feels that neutrality maximizes the possibility for growth of the individual's resources. The critics of neutrality feel it to be dehumanizing and to lead to sterile, intellectualized, noninteraction. The exposed, or "nude," therapist, who exposes himself psychologically or physically, claims to be emotionally stimulating and humanistic. Neutrals regard therapists who touch their patients and expose both skin and psyche as, at best, indulging in mutual mental masturbation and, at worst, in fornication.[9]

I will now examine, in some detail, the technical aspects of use of self as seen from several widely disparate schools of psychotherapeutic theory and practice: psychoanalysis, existential psychotherapy, humanistic psychology, marathon group psychotherapy, and behavorial therapy.

PSYCHOANALYSIS

Psychoanalysis aims to modify personality structure through introspection, based on the premise that the greater one's awareness of his unconscious ego defense mechanisms and of his unconscious fantasies, the freer one is to deal with reality. Symptomatology is seen as the end-product of the ego's defense against anxiety, which in turn signals the presence of unconscious conflict. The treatment process is the development and resolution of the transference neurosis. The resolution comes through interpretation of the transference neurosis.

The analyst's use of himself as a person begins with Freud. The "wolf man," Freud's famous analysand of 1910–1914, recalled several self-disclosures made by Freud:

> Once during an analytic hour Freud told me that he had just received word that his youngest son had broken a leg skiing, but that luckily it was a mild injury with no danger of lasting damage. Freud went on to say that of his three sons the youngest was most like him in character and temperament.[10]

On at least one occasion, Freud spoke about another of his patients to the wolf man.[11] Freud lent money to him,[12] complimented him by saying that it would be good if all his pupils could grasp analysis as well as the wolf man,[13] and gave his opinions on literature from time to time.[14] So as not to overstate Freud's willingness to disclose himself to the wolf man during the latter's four-year analysis and brief reanalysis, let me quote the wolf man again:

> too close a relationship between patient and doctor has, like everything else in life, its shadow side. Freud himself believed that if the friendly relations between the two overstep a certain boundary, this will work against the therapy.[15]

Freud discussed with the wolf man neither the loss of his own daughter at their appointment on the day after her death nor the pain he (Freud) suffered from the numerous surgical procedures he underwent while still acquainted with the wolf man.[16]

Freud's openness with the wolf man reassured the latter of his worth as a person to Freud, but it also gave rise to a notion of himself as a favorite son, which in turn blocked working through his negative feelings toward his father and Freud. This bit of residual transference was analyzed successfully when he later sought treatment from Freud and was referred to Ruth Mack Brunswick. Brunswick punctured the wolf man's idea of himself as Freud's favorite patient by telling him bluntly that Freud had left the treatment in her hands and that Freud displayed no unusual interest in the case. This enabled him to experience his formerly unconscious rage toward Freud as a father-surrogate.[17]

Freud took a dim view of Sandor Ferenczi's experiments with more "active" techniques that involved expressions of affection and physical contact with patients in an effort to help them reexperience more positively their earlier relationships with their parents. This presumably helped to neutralize the patients' earlier unhappiness and emotional deprivation. To what extent the feelings Ferenczi demonstrated to his patients were real and to what extent he was engaged in role playing, we cannot know. Freud wrote angrily:

> You have not made a secret of the fact that you kiss your patients and let them kiss you; I had also heard that from a patient of my own. Now when you decide to give a full account of your technique and its results you will have to choose between two ways: either you relate this or you conceal it. The latter, as you may well think, is dishonorable. What one does in one's technique one has to defend openly. Besides, both ways soon come together. Even if you don't say so yourself it will soon get known, just as I knew it before you told me.
>
> Now I am assuredly not one of those who from prudishness or from considerations of bourgeois convention would condemn little erotic gratifications of this kind. And I am also aware that in the time of Nibelungs a kiss was a harmless greeting granted to every guest . . . But that does not alter the fact . . . that with us a kiss signifies a certain erotic intimacy. We have hitherto in our technique held to the conclusion that patients are to be refused erotic gratifications . . .
>
> Now picture what will be the result of publishing your technique. There is no revolutionary who is not driven out of the field by a still more radical one. A number of independent thinkers in matters of technique will say to themselves: Why stop at a kiss? Certainly one gets further when one adopts "pawing" as well, which after all doesn't make a baby.

And then bolder ones will come along who will go further, to peeping and showing—and soon we shall have accepted in the technique of analysis the whole repertoire of demiviergerie and petting parties, resulting in an enormous increase of interest in psychoanalysis, among both analysts and patients. The new adherent, however, will easily claim too much of this interest for himself; the younger of our colleagues will find it hard to stop at the point they originally intended, and God the Father, Ferenczi, gazing at the lively scene he has created will perhaps say to himself: Maybe after all I should have halted in my technique of motherly affection before the kiss.[17]

Freud was obviously aware of the potentiality for both therapist and patient to exploit the treatment situation for personal satisfaction other than the resolution of neurotic problems. In 1912, he made specific suggestions on self-disclosure by the analyst.

The young and eager psychoanalyst will certainly be tempted to bring his own individuality freely into the discussion, in order to draw out the patient and help him over the confines of his narrow personality. One would expect it to be entirely permissible, and even desirable, for the overcoming of the patients' resistances, that the physician should afford him a glimpse into his own life. One confidence repays another, and anyone demanding intimate revelations from another must be prepared to make them himself.

But the psycho-analytic relationship is a thing apart; much of it takes a different course from that which the psychology of consciousness would lead us to expect. Experience [Freud must have tried it!] does not bear witness to the excellence of an affective technique of this kind. Further, it . . . verges on treatment by suggestion. It will induce the patient to bring forward sooner and with less difficulty what he already knows and would otherwise have kept back for a time on account of conventional objections. But this technique achieves nothing towards the discovering of the patient's unconscious; it makes him less able than ever to overcome the deeper resistances and in the more severe cases it invariably fails on account of the insatiability it rouses in the patient, who then tries to reverse the situation, finding the analysis of the physician more interesting than his own. The loosening of the transference, too—one of the main tasks of the cure is made more difficult by too intimate an attitude on the part of the doctor, so that a doubtful gain in the beginning is more than cancelled in the end.[19]

Psychoanalysts currently maintain a spectrum of attitudes toward self-disclosure. Menninger has stated with regard to touching that "transgressions of the rule against physical contact constitute . . . evidence of the incompetence or criminal ruthlessness of the analyst."[20] Rosenfeld maintains strict neutrality. He regards all productions of the patient as primarily transference determined and deals with them by interpretation.[21] Greenson maintains that civility toward the patient, compassion for his plight, respect for him as a human being, recognition of the patient's achievements in therapy, and acknowledgment of the analyst's own lapses when they become visible to the patient are vital ingredients of the treatment situation. He sees them as beyond transference and interpretation and feels they are more difficult, if not impossible, to teach.[22] His last point contrasts with the views of Carkhuff, which will be elaborated below. Alger suggests an even more egalitarian stand in which the analyst shares more of his moment-to-moment feelings with the patient, thus stimulating greater openness by the patient.[23]

EXISTENTIAL PSYCHOTHERAPY
To the analytic notion of neurotic anxiety, existentialism adds the concept of ontic anxiety: a being's awareness of its own finitude, its inevitable nonbeing or death.[24] Neurosis, in existential terms, is an avoidance of the despair of nonbeing by avoiding being, i.e., by avoiding facing the reality of one's finiteness and by taking refuge in symptoms.[25]

The existential approach deemphasizes technical procedures so that the existential therapist will not deal with people as objects to be manipulated, managed, or analyzed. It deals with symptoms as limitations of the patient's being-in-the-world, sees transference in terms of limited and restricted experiencing of others, repression and resistance as unwillingness to accept the freedom of one's potentialities. The existential therapist is a full human presence—not a reflector. He sees his patients through participation. He is one existence communicating with another, an experience, not an explanation. Transference is dealt with in the context of a relationship between two real people, and the therapist deals with his countertransference in order to be more fully present rather than to be better able to objectify his patient.[26]

The technical processes of existential psychotherapy are termed *being, keeping looking,* and *staying. Being* is the therapist's attempt to enter the emotional life of his patient through an empathic process. *Keeping looking* means regarding the patient as an open, changing system. *Staying* refers to the therapist dealing with his own feelings to reduce the emotional distance between himself and a patient. For example, an existential therapist expresses his anger with a patient, not for the sake of expressing it but for the sake of reaching or remaining with the patient. The existential method seeks a relationship that becomes so valuable to both parties that they are willing to change in order to preserve it.[27]

Whitaker and Malone, in 1953, proposed a more radical confrontation between therapist and patient as real people living in the here and now. They constructed a theoretical course of psychotherapy in which,

the young therapist is told never to verbalize without affect. Words which are not reinforced by personal feeling are not pertinent in psychotherapy . . . the young therapist is told never to interpret content, which is presented by the patient with deep feeling, but to relate, as a person, with feeling to each symbol presented by the patient . . . physical contact is a technical aid in the therapeutic process . . . holding the patient during a crying episode, or offering to rock the patient during a period of deep regression into infantile living brings to the therapeutic relationship certain proprioceptive and sensory modulations which make a significant contribution to the therapeutic process.[28]

HUMANISTIC PSYCHOLOGY

The humanistic psychology movement began in part as a reaction against the "dehumanizing" neutrality of the psychoanalytic therapist.

The focus of this movement is away from psychopathology and toward human potential. The person seeking help is not sick but is seeking to fulfill his potential in relation to himself and others. Thus, the goal is personal growth rather than resolution of conflict or emotional ills. Individuals are regarded as having a positive drive toward greater self-fulfillment, which the therapist seeks to facilitate. This does not require the working through of defenses; defenses reflect the ineptness of the therapist in helping his patient find the optimal conditions for growth. The patient's growth is stimulated by contact with the real person of the therapist.

Jourard, one of the early advocates of openness with patients, suggests a need for transparency on the part of the therapist. By transparency, he means an openness to one's inner and outer world, and a willingness to disclose one's self to others.[29] Jourard bases his therapeutic approach on questionnaire studies and experimental interviews with volunteer subjects that indicate that people are more open with interviewers who are self-disclosing than with interviewers who reveal little about themselves.[30] He extrapolated from the experimental interview situation to the process of psychotherapy and recommended that "the most effective way to invite authentic disclosure from another is to take the risky lead and offer it oneself."[31]

Carkhuff elaborated a concept of *genuineness* from the work of Rogers (see below) that includes self-disclosure by the therapist. Genuineness is the ability of the helper to be freely, spontaneously, and deeply himself, disclosing significant information about himself when appropriate. He sees this as directly related to the patient's ability to be genuine and self-disclosing in appropriate relationships.[32]

Carkhuff devised a rating scale of genuineness and proposed a method by which therapists in training can become more genuine. This is accomplished through direct observation of helper-helpee interactions in which the helper (therapist) is rated on his degree of genuineness and is given suggestions to help him emit more genuine responses to his patients. The problem with this technique is that the helper-therapist may not become more in touch with himself. Rather, he may become more expert at simulating genuineness. Simulated genuineness is an affront to the patient's sensibilities. It contradicts the patient's intuitive awareness that the therapist is merely acting a part and helps to undermine the patient's reality testing.

Truax utilizes the concept of genuineness and includes in it the terms *acting oneself* and *being integrated, authentic,* and *nondefensive.* He sees the therapist as needing to operate without defensive phoniness and without hiding behind a professional facade or other role.[33]

Rogers refers to the self-disclosing therapist as *congruent.* He defines congruence as being what one is in one's relationship with a client: "being without facade and openly being the feelings and attitudes currently flowing within himself."[34] Rogers illustrates his concept of congruence in his film, *Journey into Self.* The film consists of excerpts from a weekend marathon group in which Rogers sheds tears and expresses affection toward one of the group members.[35] Rogers' congruence is one of a triad of therapist-offered conditions, the other two being accurate empathy and nonpossessive warmth. Rogers feels that these three therapist-offered conditions are the primary tools of any therapist, regardless of his theoretical orientation.

BEHAVIORAL THERAPY

Bandura challenges the view of normal human development as the acquisition of new response patterns through a shaping process involving selective reinforcement of trial-and-error performances.[36] He argues that such a process is inefficient and hardly conducive to learning the innumerable complex tasks that must be mastered in the course of human maturation. From his research, Bandura concludes that new patterns of behavior in the developing child are acquired observationally without a laborious response-shaping process. Response elements are organized into new patterns of behavior at a symbolic level on the basis of information conveyed by modeling stimuli.

Bandura criticizes conventional interview treatments in which therapists mainly engage in silence and interpretive behaviors that have little direct value for altering behavior. Modeling theory suggests that one can best become what one is shown how to be: modeling is better for overcoming social inhibitions than providing a permissive atmosphere and waiting for the desired behavior to emerge.

The concepts propounded by Bandura fit well into the framework of behavioral therapy, which deals with emotional symptoms as learned behavior that can be altered by determining the conditions that serve as reinforcers, eliminating the reinforcers, and supplying means to acquire more adaptive substitute behaviors by direct teaching with appropriate rewards to reinforce the more desirable new behaviors. Behavioral techniques are employed in many therapeutic contexts, especially in the more directive approaches.

Modeling (offering some aspect of one's self as a model for iden- tification) plays an important part in behavioral techniques, in the ex- tinction of undesirable behaviors, and in the acquisition of more desir- able behaviors. Frequently, the behavior modeled by the therapist is one the patient fears to undertake. Sometimes it is simply not within his social repertoire. Behavioral therapists feel that imitation of the therapist, if adequately reinforced, can lead to relatively stable changes in behavior. Assertiveness training is a good example of such a tech- nique. The patient imitates assertive behavior modeled by the therapist. As he begins to feel more assertive in the process, he receives the appro- bation of the therapist and is also reinforced by the positive changes he is able to bring about in his own life.

MARATHON GROUP PSYCHOTHERAPY
Marathon group psychotherapists adopted the concept of openness on the rationale that the group leader provides a role model for the mem- bers of his group. Rachman states that the marathon group therapist not only leads but also enters into the group interaction in the same way as the participants, exposing himself to the scrutiny of the group.[37]

Mintz, a psychologist with psychoanalytic training, feels that therapy is essentially a one-sided relationship and therefore reveals her feelings and shares her own experiences only insofar as she judges they will be therapeutically helpful.[38]

Robertiello, a psychoanalytically trained psychiatrist, reports that he is completely open with members of his therapy groups, shares both his feelings and his problems, and looks to the members of his group for help with his own personal problems.[39]

Jacques Levy, the psychologist who conceived and directed the nude review *Oh! Calcutta,* made the following remarks (reminiscent of Freud's comments to Ferenczi) in an address delivered to the American Group Psychotherapy Association in February, 1971.

I have not come here today to tell you to stop. There is an old Western saying: "Faint heart never filled a flush." But in the context of professionalism there are few poker players. Maybe that's good. Maybe not. But for those of you who are thinking of working seriously in the area of encounter and sensitivity training . . . In the overwhelming rush to get with 'what's happening' in the encounter boom, not enough people are facing the questions squarely. And if you can't face them ahead of time when you come to that moment—it may, for all I know, be the exquisite high point of your professional career—the moment when you see an unplanned orgy about to happen before your trained eyes, you won't have to ask yourself "What's happening?" You'll know![40]

The Problem

Why the trend away from a neutral stance to one of personal openness with patients? Are we forgetting (or repressing) Freud's admonitions, beginning again to gratify transference expectations and siding with the patient's resistance to exploring his unconscious mind? Or is Freud's axiom of neutrality less applicable in nonanalytic forms of treatment? Do the existentialists and the humanists address themselves to an aspect of psychopathology hitherto ignored? Experiencing the therapist as a person is more rewarding to certain patients than experiencing him as neutral and reflective. But is it therapeutic? The personal needs of the therapist are evident through much of the material I have reviewed. Many therapists find it difficult to operate as a neutral therapeutic instrument for thirty or forty years of professional life. The personal frustration for the therapist is enormous and, in itself, a significant occupational hazard. It is literally more than many therapists can bear, especially at periods in their lives when their own object hunger is great. It is axiomatic that one should have emotional satisfaction outside of one's practice, but does this mean that the therapist must be emotionally sterile during his working hours?

Are the therapist's urges to disclose himself to patients related primarily to his own needs? To countertransference? Are disclosures basically a form of acting out? The action-oriented therapist is more likely to act out his countertransference or to deal with personal needs by projecting them onto his patient. Historically, the action-prone therapist has shown not only less self-awareness but also less capacity for self-control in his dealings with patients. Now that means of direct observation of the therapeutic process are available, more can be done to ascertain whose needs are being met.

The issues are: Can therapy gratify the human needs of both therapist and patient without compromising the patient's treatment needs? If so, what are the human needs? To what degree must they be gratified to maintain the treatment process? To what extent must they be frustrated to facilitate treatment? Beyond the need for a humanized interaction, does clinical experience and a review of the literature suggest indications and contraindications to self-disclosure by the therapist?

References

1. Descartes, René: Discourse on method. In *Modern Classical Philosophers.* B. Rand, ed. Houghton Mifflin, Boston, 1936, pp. 101–116.

2. Hegel, G. W.: The doctrine of essence. In Rand, *op. cit.* pp. 592–594.

3. Tillich, P.: *The Courage to Be.* Yale University Press, New Haven, 1952, p. 124.

4. May, R., Angel, E., and Ellenberger, H. F. *Existence.* Basic Books, New York, 1958, p. 11.

5. Sullivan, H. S.: *The Psychiatric Interview.* W. W. Norton, New York, 1954, p. 3.

6. May et al., *op. cit.* pp. 37–92.

7. Rogers, C. R.: The necessary and sufficient conditions of therapeutic personality change. *J. Consult. Psychol.* 21:95–103, 1957.

8. Rogers, C. R.: *On Becoming a Person.* Houghton Mifflin, Boston, 1961.

9. Weiner, M. F.: Nudity versus neutrality in psychotherapy. Presented at the First Annual Institute of the Golden Gate Group Psychotherapy Society, June, 1969.

10. Gardiner, M., ed. *The Wolf Man.* Basic Books, New York, 1971, p. 144.

11. Ibid., p. 142.

12. Ibid.

13. Ibid.

14. Ibid., pp. 145–146.

15. Ibid., p. 141.

16. Ibid., p. 157.

17. Ibid., p. 284.

18. Jones, E.: *Life and Work of Sigmund Freud,* Vol. III. Basic Books, New York, 1957, pp. 163–164.

19. Freud, S.: Recommendations for physicians on the psychoanalytic method of treatment, 1923. In *Collected Papers of Sigmund Freud,* Vol. 2. Basic Books, New York, 1959, pp. 323–333.

20. Menninger, K.: *Theory of Psychoanalytic Technique.* Basic Books, New York, 1958, p. 40.

21. Rosenfeld, H. A.: *Psychotic States: A Psychoanalytic Approach.* International Universities Press, New York, 1965.

22. Greenson, R. R.: Beyond transference and interpretation, *Internat. J. Psychoanal.* 53:213–217, 1972.

23. Alger, I.: Freedom in analytic therapy. *Curr. Psychiatr. Ther.* 9:73–78, 1969.

24. Tillich, P.: *op. cit.,* p. 35.

25. Ibid., p. 66.

26. May, R.: Contributions of existential psychotherapy. In *Existence.* R. May, E. Angel, and H. F. Ellenberger, eds. Basic Books, New York, 1958, pp. 37–91.

27. Havens, L. L.: The existential use of the self. *Am. J. Psychiatry* 131:1–10, 1974.

28. Whitaker, C. A., and Malone, T. P.: *The Roots of Psychotherapy.* Blakiston, New York, 1953.

29. Jourard, S. M.: *Self-Disclosure, An Experimental Analysis of the Transparent Self.* Wiley-Interscience, New York, 1971, p. 38.

30. Jourard, S. M., and Resnick, J. L.: Some effects of self-disclosure among college women, *J. Humanist. Psychol.* 10:84–93, 1970.

31. Jourard, S. M.: *op. cit.,* p. 184.

32. Carkhuff, R. R.: *Helping and Human Relations,* Vol. I. Holt, Rinehart and Winston, New York, 1969, p. 38.

33. Truax, C. B.: Research in certain therapists' interpersonal skills in relation to process and outcome. In *Handbook of Psychotherapy and Behavior Change.* Bergin, A. F. and Garfield, S. L., eds. John Wiley, New York, 1971, pp. 299–344.

34. Rogers, C. R.: *On Becoming a Person.* Houghton Mifflin, Boston, 1961, p. 61.

35. Rogers, C. R.: *Journey Into Self,* film, 1968, Western Behavioral Science Institute, La Jolla, California.

36. Bandura, A.: Psychotherapy based on modeling principles. In *Handbook of Psychotherapy and Behavior Change.* Bergin, A. E., and Garfield, S. L. eds. John Wiley, New York, 1971.

37. Rachman, A. W.: Marathon group psychotherapy: its origins, significance and direction, *J. Group Psychoanal. Pro.* 2:57–74, 1969–1970.

38. Mintz, E. E.: *Marathon Groups: Reality and Symbol.* Appleton-Century-Crofts, New York, 1971, pp. 29–30.

39. Robertiello, R. C.: The leader in a "leaderless" group. *Psychother. Theo. Res. Prac.* 9:259–261, 1972.

40. Levy, J.: Group responses to simulated erotic experiences in a theatrical production. *Internat. J. Group Psychother.* 21:275–287, 1971.

3.

What Is Use of Self?

One's self is the constantly changing product of one's thoughts, feelings, life experiences, genetic makeup, and physiological state. No one can fully know himself, and no one can fully expose his self to another. To introduce use of self as a therapeutic instrument, let us take the task of helping a woman to deal with feelings about her mother's death. An impersonal therapist would say, "What did you feel?" or, "You must have had some feeling reaction!" or simply, "Tell me about it." Thus, he indicates technical expertise and willingness to deal with the patient's feelings. A personal therapist displays concern, empathizes, or tells of a similar experience in addition to applying his technical expertise. The disclosing therapist says, "It's difficult for me to believe that you had no reaction to your mother's death. I know how strongly I feel at funerals, even if I'm not related to the dead person." By sharing his personal reactions, the therapist heightens emotional awareness.

The manner, style, purpose, emotional demand met, and aspect of himself that a therapist reveals are important. This chapter illustrates the varieties of use of self and includes an estimate of the probable impact of each disclosure. A therapeutic intervention is rarely followed by an immediate, dramatic reaction. It is usually one link in a chain of therapeutic events which results in emotional growth, therapeutic stalemate, or worsening of the patient's condition. In many instances, the absence of a negative occurrence—a suicide attempt or premature termination of treatment—is the only sign of an appropriate intervention.[1]

Manner

One may disclose one's self by word or by act, consciously or unconsciously.

Mrs. A., a patient with whom I had good rapport, noted that I was emotionally withdrawn during one session. She asked if I was reacting to her. Rather than answer her question with a question, I elected to self-disclose. I acknowledged my emotional withdrawal and said that I had just been angered by an event unrelated to her. She accepted my explanation, and her therapy continued without setback. I disclosed in preference to reflecting her question because I felt I could undercut her sense that she caused whatever happened around her. I also felt that "owning up" to my emotional situation would validate her reality testing and help her to become more reliant on her own judgment.

I used physical contact successfully with another patient.

I had worked intermittently with Mr. D., a 25-year-old man, for five years. During one session, in response to his request, I sat with him on my couch, held his hand, and allowed him to literally cry on my shoulder. Previously, he had worked through some homosexual fantasies about me and was beginning to separate me, in his mind, from his deceased mother, whom he had seen as cold, ungiving, and controlling. Several weeks later, when the distortion arose again, I cited this time of physical intimacy to correct his distorted perception of me.

Purpose

Use of self transmits information about the therapist as a person. Some disclosures are important orienting information; the patient is entitled to know his therapist's professional qualifications, his therapeutic orientation, the general approach he intends to take, and his rationale.

Of greater importance in psychotherapy is the instrumental use of self, in which disclosures are intended to have a specific impact on the patient. The disclosure to Mrs. A., above, demonstrates deliberate instrumental disclosure.

Unconsciously determined disclosures may have significant, although "accidental," instrumental effects. Through them, patients often become aware of therapists' attitudes and feelings. My disclosure to Mrs. A. had the further effect of indicating my concern about her as a person.

Many self-disclosures can only be classified as informational or instrumental in retrospect, based on the reactions of the patient. In all instances, they must be considered in terms of the patient's feelings about the therapist and the therapist's feelings toward the patient.

Style

The type and process of self-disclosure varies with different people and different contexts. For each therapist they are highly variable, complex, and can be understood only by prolonged observation in different frames of reference. Through repeated self-observation, a therapist can become aware of his style. Modern videotape equipment can readily be adapted to an office of ordinary size and requires little technical expertise to operate.[2] The degree and style of a therapist's self-disclosures frequently transcend his theoretical orientation and his conscious intent. A therapist who sees himself as neutral may appear sarcastic and demeaning on videotape; another, who feels open and spontaneous, may appear contrived and mechanical. The therapist's style reflects his personality as much as his theoretical orientation. From observing his style objectively, the therapist can better appreciate his personal needs and idiosyncrasies, and their impact on patients.

Videotape recordings are most useful when viewed with a peer or a supervisor. In some cases, it is useful to review the tape with the patient involved. Videotapes are less useful when reviewed by the therapist alone, because he is blind to his prejudices and emotional difficulties unless he has had adequate training, supervision, and personal therapy.

Changes in style with different patients and during the course of any one patient's therapy may be a useful index of the therapist's feelings about the patient and vice versa. When cotherapists work in group or family therapy, changes in style may stem from shifts in the cotherapists' relationship. These changes in style often reflect unconscious reactions to patients. Objectifying the changes gives the therapist greater opportunity to recognize the role of his countertransference feelings.

Demand

The demand for use of self as a therapeutic instrument arises in the therapist, the patient, or the relationship between them. Many therapists feel a strong need to expose and make use of their personalities in the therapeutic process; abstinence renders these individuals less authentic. The therapist must determine if it is more important to be authentic or to suppress himself and emphasize technical operations. When the therapist feels impelled to disclose, there is danger of an unconscious collusion to avoid talking about the patient. There is also danger that the therapist is exploiting the therapy situation to meet his own needs. The patient may have less need for his therapist as a person than as an effective therapeutic instrument.[3]

Some patients vigorously demand that the therapist expose himself as a person. This is rare with well-integrated, highly motivated patients. The persons who most strongly press for human interaction tend to use therapy to perpetuate maladaptive behavior rather than to examine it. Several of my patients have terminated therapy because I would not become sexually or romantically involved with them. The case of Mrs. L., which follows, illustrates how a patient with little motivation to change can manipulate a therapist by demanding openness.

Types of Self-Disclosure

FEELINGS

Therapists have been encouraged by many authors to disclose their feelings concerning the patient during the therapy hour. Rogers and Truax describe the context in which they feel it appropriate for the therapist to express here-and-now feelings.

> so if I sense that I am feeling bored by my contacts with the client and the feeling persists, I think I owe it to him and to our relationship to share this feeling with him. The same would hold if my feeling is one of being afraid of the client ... But as I attempt to share these feelings I also want to be constantly in touch with what is going on in me. If I can, I will recognize that it is my feeling of being bored that I am exposing, and not some supposed fact about him as a boring person. If I voice it as my own reaction, it has the potentiality of leading to a deep relationship. But this feeling exists in the context of a complex and changing flow, and this needs to be communicated, too. I would like to share with him my distress at feeling bored

and the discomfort I feel in expressing this aspect of me. As I face this attitude I find that my feeling of boredom arises from my sense of remoteness from him and that I would like to be more in touch with him and even as I try to express these feelings they change. I am certainly not bored as I wait with eagerness and perhaps a bit of apprehension for his response. I also feel a new sensitivity to him now that I have bared this feeling which has been a barrier between us. I am very much more able to hear the surprise or perhaps the hurt in his voice as he now finds himself speaking more genuinely because I have dared to be real to him. I have let myself be a person—real, imperfect—in my relationship with him.[4]

The following self-disclosures are from my own practice.

In Mrs. E.'s second session of individual psychotherapy, she claimed I was inconsiderate because I left my briefcase on the chair where she wanted to sit. I suggested that she return to the chair in which she sat the first time. She said, "I expect freedom in here, and there is none!" I was caught off guard and responded sarcastically. As we discussed this interaction later in the session, I said that she had angered me with her remark. At our next session, she said that in view of my angry response, she felt I was not a good psychiatrist. By this time, I had become aware that she was encouraging me to hurt her, but no amount of dispassionate interpretation could salvage the day. She called me before her next session, said she did not feel she could work with me, and we agreed for her to seek further help elsewhere, if she wished to continue in treatment. In this situation, there was insufficient alliance between the patient's capacity to observe herself objectively and my ability to make rational observations without taking action. Her attack against me elicited a counterattack. I, in effect, had sided with the destructively self-critical aspect of her.

When strongly impelled to reveal their feelings, therapists are often in emotional conflict about the patient. Rather than immediately disclose, it is useful to refrain and listen further to the patient. This precludes the therapist's avoidance of some aspect of the patient by disclosing himself. At other times, a disclosure expresses, or is a reaction to, feelings about the patient. With Mrs. L., it was an instrument to sidetrack me.

Mrs. L., an attractive woman with whom I had worked individually for several years, entered a group concomitant with her individual therapy. The situation was highly unfavorable. She had been pushed into treatment by her husband. Shortly after beginning individual therapy, she was able to shift the situation in such a way that I frequently talked more than she during our sessions. She insisted that our situation was unfair and put considerable pressure on me to talk about myself and my own feelings. I acquiesced and told her of my attraction to her and my feelings that we were alike in several respects, to add to the humanness of our situation.

Six months after she began combined therapy, our individual sessions were still unproductive. Accordingly, I suggested that we discontinue them and continue with the group sessions. She readily agreed, but in the next group session vehemently attacked me and cited my disclosures as examples of my incompetence. She said she had seen another psychiatrist and that her husband was contemplating a malpractice suit against me based on my personal revelations and my termination of her individual therapy without adequate preparation. She wrote a letter of apology addressed to the group but called me afterward to say that she would return to the group only if I withheld the letter from the group. In short, I was to allow her to be abusive and uncooperative so that she would not have to examine her behavior. I refused, and she terminated treatment angrily.

My sessions with this woman had been painful, trying experiences for me. My guilt over my attraction to her made it difficult for me to deal with her uncooperativeness. In spite of having obtained consultation, I was not able to help her see that she had invested most of her energy in therapy evading herself. My rejection precipitated an overt display of the rage that she had manifested previously by uncooperativeness.

ATTITUDES AND OPINIONS

Mrs. F., who was nearing the end of several years of intensive psychotherapy, asked my attitude toward the people with whom I had seen her at a social event. I told her my reaction to them, based on my past social interactions with them. At the next session, she said she finally understood the message I had been trying to get across to her for a long time—that many of her relationships were based on social prestige rather than the meaning of others for her as a person. Her recognition of my attitude first brought it to my own awareness. Therapy continued in a positive manner. She had grown emotionally to a point where she could perceive and react to my attitude as neutral data rather than as a condemnation. She accepted it without berating herself or having to work through several layers of defensive reactions.

Patients frequently ask my opinion of books written for professional or lay audiences. When appropriate, I say what I think is worthwhile in a book and what is not. From time to time, I recommend readings that fit a particular patient's needs. I have encouraged some patients who experience difficulty in coping from day to day to read Abraham Low's book, *Mental Health through Will Training*.[5] To obese patients interested in losing weight, I suggest that Weight Watchers has more to offer than any other form of psychotherapy for weight control per se.

Often, when strongly tempted to reveal my attitudes and opinions, I am reinforcing my omniscient authority and the patient's sense of helplessness. Therapists promote this type of relationship by statements like, "I think you should . . . " (implying the therapist knows best) or "I think the real problem is . . ." (implying the patient's perception is incorrect). When the therapist wishes to emphasize his authority, however, such exposures may be entirely appropriate.

Some situations call for expert opinion. If a patient requires hospitalization, the therapist must say so. If medication is an appropriate adjunctive measure, the therapist must suggest it and tell the patient what he can expect as therapeutic gain as well as side effects. One gives advice to patients in long-term supportive therapy where one is a permanent auxiliary ego. Rarely, in my own practice, I give my opinion about the chances of success of a marital situation.[6]

FORMULATIONS AND INTERPRETATTIONS

A formulation is an attempt to relate together the thoughts, feelings, behavior, and history of a patient. Formulations are useful intellectual handles that enable the therapist to communicate a complicated conceptualization in a shorthand manner. They deal with material readily available to the patient's consciousness, while helping him to view this material from a different frame of reference. An interpretation, by contrast, is a type of formulation that brings formerly unconscious material to consciousness. Generally, what is revealed about the therapist by his formulations and interpretations is his professional orientation and training rather than his person.

ASSOCIATIONS

To associate is to temporarily suspend rational thinking and allow the unconscious links among thoughts, feelings, and behavior to emerge. Disclosing an association reveals some aspect of the therapist's unconscious, but sharing isolated associations ordinarily reveals little about the therapist and can be used to help patients learn to associate or to help patients who are temporarily blocked.

Miss E. was concerned about the homosexual implications of a dream she had about another woman, whom she knew only vaguely. I asked the woman's name. My patient responded, and I said, "That's my name!" She had frequently heard me addressed in this manner but could not connect the woman and me. As we talked further, it became clear that the dream reflected her wish for and fear of closeness with me.

At other times, revealing my associations is less useful, in that it reinforces the attitude that my associations are right while the patient's are inadequate or wrong. Patients' dependence on the therapist's associations can help obstruct awareness of their unconscious processes and reinforce their sense of inadequacy.

FANTASIES

Disclosure of the therapist's fantasies allows the patient to enter his inner world. Searles reports the following interesting incident from the treatment of a severely regressed, institutionalized, schizophrenic patient.

> One hebephrenic woman kept trying to get me to elope with her to Florida and in various ways chided me for being so stodgy. In one session I sensed, with relief, that she was trying merely to get me to unbend and share such an experience with her in fantasy, whereupon I confessed, "Well, if you're thinking of this in terms of fantasy, I've already had intercourse with you several times in fantasy so far this hour!" To this she responded, with such pleasure as I had rarely seen in our often despair-filled years of work, "Progress has been made in this room!"[7]

EXPERIENCES

Therapists do not commonly share experiences from outside their relationships with a given patient or group. They do, however, utilize experiences they have had with a particular patient or group as a frame of reference, or a benchmark, to measure progress or regression.

I occasionally bring in personal experiences to validate a patient's reality testing, especially when my efficiency has been impaired. Shortly before one group session, a close friend called to tell me that his wife had died a few hours before. Although nearly paralyzed, I decided not to cancel the group session because there was no way to notify the members. During the session, I told of my sense of loss and my feeling of numbness. The therapeutic process was temporarily impaired, but we were able to resume during the next session, in which several of the patients expressed fear of my vulnerability.

NUDITY

Nudity is only sometimes a form of self-disclosure. Bindrim has conducted marathon group therapy sessions in the nude since 1968.[8] He uses a highly structured format, including music, special lighting effects, and a swimming pool. His group members have found physical nudity helpful to overcome shame and embarrassment about their bodies. Although nude himself, Bindrim discloses little more of his person than if he were fully clothed.

PHYSICAL CONTACT

There is considerable pressure on therapists to have physical contact with their patients. [9, 10] Patients want an experience of closeness and warmth as expressed through bodily contact, not physical contact per se. Some are interested in sexual gratification or various kinds of transference gratification. It is difficult to know under what circumstances the therapist's feelings are best communicated verbally, through gesture, or through physical contact. When a relatively well-integrated outpatient makes a concerted push for physical contact, the contact will more likely distract from therapy rather than facilitate communication.

Therapists can also experience considerable pressure from within themselves to have physical contact with patients. I ordinarily limit my contact to a handshake on first meeting the patient and an occasional handshake after vacations. I have hugged several patients at times of mutually strong, positive feelings. I perform superficial physical examinations, such as a blood-pressure check, when the situation warrants. Otherwise, I allow the patient to take the lead in physical contact. Physical contact with a patient, while not itself a self-disclosure, may reveal an aspect of the therapist that is detrimental to the patient. A patient's illusion that his therapist is a warm, comfortable person may be devastatingly dispelled by an awkward, stiff return of an embrace by the therapist. An aggressive, overly enthusiastic physical contact may suggest that the therapist is more needy of contact than the patient.

Physical contact can have either a positive or a negative impact.

In response to her request, I attempted to communicate warmth and caring to Mrs. B. by holding her hand during the therapeutic hour. She had been in treatment with me for several years, during which time she had required hospitalization twice. Between hospitalizations, she was barely compensated psychologically. Attempting to physically communicate my feelings only intensified her regression.[11]

This, as well as other similar experiences with expressing feelings through physical contact, suggests that it is most strongly demanded by the individuals who have the least capacity to constructively integrate it. There may be severe, regressive consequences in individuals with limited coping ability.

HISTORY AND OTHER PERSONAL DATA

Patients occasionally ask my age, place of birth, and religion. I usually ask why they want to know. This gives me a clue about the patient's wishes and needs. If a patient's therapeutic needs are best served by knowing about me as a real person, I will accede to a request for historical information. If asking for such information is a defensive tactic, I abstain. To avoid experiences like the following, one should refrain from unsolicited disclosures.

Early in his therapy with me, Mr. E. asked my religion. I told him that I am Jewish. I volunteered that I belong to a Reform congregation. He said he understood that Reform Jews are liberals. I did not respond to this but said that my congregation was housed in a Methodist church widely known for its liberal leanings. He was aghast. He was an ultraconservative, and his ability to work with me was severely impaired until he and I became comfortable with our religious and political differences.

On the other hand, certain disclosures are unavoidable.

In February 1972, I suffered an acute myocardial infarction while in New York City, and I was unable to return to my home in Dallas for a month. My secretary was initially told to cancel the following week's appointments. A few days later, when I was certain that I would need to remain at the hospital approximately four weeks, I instructed my secretary to cancel my appointments until further notice and to tell my patients I had suffered a mild coronary and would be returning to practice as soon as I was able.

When I began to see my patients again, I reviewed their reactions to my illness. None of the patients who continued with me was overwhelmed by the information. However, two patients discontinued therapy; one of them found it impossible to arrange a convenient time, although her former time was offered. The other transferred to another therapist. Mrs. B. attempted briefly to spare me stress by minimizing her difficulties. Mrs. A. stated, both angrily and acceptingly, that I had again proved myself a human being instead of the superman she wished me to be. Some persons pressed for details about the time, place, nature of the experience, and its impact on me. I responded to the degree I felt appropriate in each case.

I saw a few patients at my home in the three weeks before I returned to the office. I continued to see patients at home in the afternoons for a month after my return to the office. More than twenty patients were asked to come to my house. One refused. Two patients who did come were markedly uncomfortable and were relieved to be able to see me at my office again. For Mrs. B., seeing me in my home surroundings was a strongly positive experience, but it reinforced her wish for a regressive closeness. In the main, there was little disruption of the therapeutic process. A number of the patients whom I have continued to see express concern about my health from time to time. Some express concern over my physical vulnerability. Others state with some satisfaction that I appear to be taking good care of myself. More than one have felt guilty about "taking" from me, but all of these expressions of concern have provided grist for the therapeutic mill.

My experiences suggest that historical information and personal data need not be excluded from the therapeutic relationship, especially concerning events that alter therapy, such as a prolonged absence of the therapist or a need to drastically revise his schedule. On the other hand, irrelevant data is best undisclosed.

RELATION TO OTHERS
The group therapist's relationship to persons other than an individual patient becomes a regular part of treatment. Group therapy involves the simultaneous relationship of the therapist with more than one patient.

The therapist must be certain that his relationship with each group member is not above discussion, even though he may need to withhold certain privileged information. The problem of outside relationships is compounded by the use of a cotherapist. Those aspects of the relationship between cotherapists that emerge in the group must be dealt with openly in the group. In a sense, the relationship between the cotherapists serves as a prototype for the group members. A mature give-and-take relationship serves as a positive model. Obvious dissimulations undermine the spirit of honesty and risk taking that is essential in group treatment.

Counseling of couples by a husband-wife professional team has come increasingly into vogue, especially in the treatment of marital sexual dysfunction.[12] To date, I have seen no reports of difficulties engendered by the relationship between the cotherapists. Because the treatment approach to sexual dysfunction is usually brief and highly structured, it is not likely that complications will arise from the cotherapists' marital relationship. In a prolonged treatment and in unstructured groups, fantasies by the patients about the husband-wife relationship play a prominent role and need to be talked out.

Exposure of the therapist's relationship to persons who do not directly enter the treatment relationship is, in most cases, a distraction from therapy. Patients frequently cannot cope with such material. If it is brought into the therapeutic relationship, the patient's reactions need to be elicited and discussed.

During Mrs. D.'s fourth year of therapy, I moved to a new office. Five months later, she commented that both offices were tastefully appointed. I told her that my wife was an interior designer. As I explored her reaction to my gratuitous exposure, I found that it rekindled her sense of inferiority for "not having done anything of worth" and reactivated feelings left over from her rivalry with her younger brother. Several weeks were required to work through the residuals of this exposure.

My relationship with Mrs. D. several years later warranted an unusual (for me) disclosure; that of my wife and my relationship to her. I had terminated with Mrs. D. after four years of three-times-a-week psychotherapy. She continued to feel dissatisfied with herself and sought treatment with another therapist, who worked with her twice a week for two years. In addition, she and her husband joined a couples' group to facilitate their communication. After a period of time in the couples' group, Mrs. D. decided to drop out and have group therapy for herself. She was referred back to me for continuation in group therapy.

In our preliminary sessions, I saw that much of her "insight" was a ruminative, obsessive defense against constructive action in her life. Accordingly, I focused on her real life in the here and now. She then made rapid strides to alter her life situation. She worked her volunteer job into a paid position. She recognized that she had used her husband's passivity to avoid seeking satisfaction for herself. He, too, had been in therapy but had made no fundamental positive change. She decided to divorce him. Soon after she instituted divorce proceedings, she discovered a mass in one breast. It was malignant. Her breast was surgically removed, and she had follow-up X-ray treatment. After five weeks of X-ray treatment, she sought an apartment of her own. (She had continued to live with her husband while receiving irradiation.) When she located a suitable apartment, she asked if I objected to her consulting with my wife, an interior designer. I did not object. Mrs. D. told my wife she was a patient of mine. My wife was impressed with Mrs. D's good taste and her emotional strength, and told her so. Mrs. D. gained significantly from the relationship; she had formerly imagined me and my wife to be superhuman. As she came to recognize that we were ordinary people with ordinary feelings and problems, she realized that she did not need to become superhuman to enjoy life. The real relationship with my wife contributed significantly to a lessening of Mrs. D's tendency to idealize others and suffer by comparison.

The preceding material reflects the variety of disclosures I have made and the variety of responses I have encountered.

Having explored the "what," "when," "where," and the impact of some of my own disclosures, I will now deal with the research findings relevant to the therapist's use of self.

Summary

The therapist may disclose himself by word or act, consciously or unconsciously. Disclosures by the therapist not only transmit information; they also affect the patient's feelings. It is useful to be aware of one's habitual style and degree of disclosure. Awareness of changes in style or in degree of disclosure can point to changes in the therapist, the patient, and their relationship.

It is of great value to note whether the pressure for therapist disclosure comes from the patient or the therapist, and to investigate it in either case.

There are many possible types of disclosure, including the therapist's current feelings in the therapy session, his attitudes and opinions, formulations and interpretations, associations, fantasies, experiences, body (visually and through physical contact), history, personal data, and relation to others involved in or outside of the therapeutic relationship.

The therapist must carefully note the effects of his disclosures to determine their usefulness and possible negative effects.

References

1. Weiner, M. F.: Levels of intervention in group psychotherapy. *Group Proc.* 3:67–81, 1970–1971.

2. Berger, M. M.: *Videotape Techniques in Psychiatric Training and Treatment.* Brunner/Mazel, New York, 1970.

3. Weiner, M. F.: Reply to Roemer, *Am. J. Psychiatry* 132:86–87, 1975.

4. Rogers, C. R., and Truax, C. D.: The therapeutic conditions antecedent to change: a theoretic view. In *The Therapeutic Relationship and Its Impact: A Study of Psychotherapy with Schizophrenics.* Rogers, C. R., Gendlin, G. T., Kiesler, D. V., and Truax, C. D., eds. University of Wisconsin Press, Madison, 1967.

5. Low, A.: *Mental Health through Will Training.* Christopher Publishing House, Boston, 1952.

6. Weiner, M. F.: "Individual" versus conjoint therapy. *Dis. Nerv. Sys.* 36:546–549, 1975.

7. Searles, H. F.: *Collected Papers on Schizophrenia and Related Subjects.* International Universities Press, New York, 1965, p. 441.

8. Bindrim, P.: A report on a nude marathon. *Psychother. Theor. Res. Prac.* 5:180–188, 1968.

9. Hollender, M. H., Luborsky, L., and Scaramella, T. J.: Body contact and sexual enticement. *AMA Arch. Gen. Psychiatry* 20:188–191, 1969.

10. Hollender, M. H.: The need or wish to be held. *AMA Arch. Gen. Psychiatry* 20:445–453, 1970.

11. Weiner, M. F.: The psychotherapeutic impasse. *Dis. Nerv. Sys.* 35:258–261, 1974.

12. Masters, W. H., and Johnson, V. E.: *Human Sexual Inadequacy.* Little, Brown, Boston, 1970.

4.

Research Studies

Quantitative studies of use of self can be grouped into two categories: *self-disclosingness* and *genuineness*. Self-disclosingness is the degree to which the therapist discloses himself to his patient(s). A therapist who states his feelings toward a patient six times during a session is quantitatively more self-disclosing than one who reveals his feelings only twice, or not at all. Genuineness is the degree that a therapist's behavior and verbalizations reflect his true values and feelings. A high degree of self-disclosingness involves a high degree of genuineness. However, a high degree of genuineness does not necessitate a high degree of self-disclosure.

The studies reported in this chapter involve both dyadic relationships and groups and include laboratory experiments with volunteers, studies of encounter groups, and studies of patients in psychotherapy.

There are few data relating use of self to outcome of psychotherapy. There are more data on the effects of self-disclosures by the therapist on the self-disclosingness of patients, which may in turn correlate with positive outcome. Much of the data from studies of psychotherapy are difficult to assess because they are from brief quasi-therapy groups of student volunteers led by naive or untrained therapists rather than designated patients in treatment with experienced, well-trained therapists.

Experiments with Nonpatients

The studies on the effects of self-disclosure by one person to another in social and laboratory settings report the effects of disclosingness (openness, or willingness to be known) rather than the effects of specific disclosures.

STUDIES OF DISCLOSINGNESS

Jourard selected twenty-four women, twelve designated as high-disclosers and twelve as low-disclosers, from eighty female undergraduates on the basis of a forty-item self-disclosure questionnaire. The low-disclosers revealed less to their partners than did the high-disclosers when dyads were formed with like-disclosing pairs. When "lows" were paired with "highs," the "highs" remained high-disclosing and the "lows" significantly increased their self-disclosures to partners.[1]

Drag found that in a laboratory setting, the relationship between experimenter and subject is an important determinant of the subject's self-disclosure as reported in questionnaires and in actual dialogue. When the experimenter was open with subject, the subject tended to be more trusting and more open at a deeply personal level than when the experimenter remained impersonal.[2]

Powell, in twenty-minute interviews with undergraduate students, found that subjects made more self-references when he matched the interviewees' self-referring statements with statements about his own related thoughts, feelings, or experiences.[3]

Jourard administered a fifteen-item self-disclosure questionnaire on an individual basis to the dean and eight faculty members of a college of nursing. Jourard found that if a subject had both disclosed much and knew much about a colleague, the other, also, knew much, and had disclosed much in turn.[4]

These data suggest that in the laboratory and in ordinary situations, self-disclosingness by one person begets or augments self-disclosure by another.

STUDIES OF CONTENT

Shapiro, Krauss, and Truax administered a questionnaire to thirty-six undergraduates, thirty-nine police applicants, and twenty hospital outpatients. They asked for a rating of the degree of genuineness, empathy, and warmth experienced from each parent and from the individuals' two closest friends. The subjects also completed a scale measuring their own disclosingness of feelings to each of these persons. The data analysis suggested a higher degree of disclosure to the persons who exhibited the greatest genuineness, empathy, and warmth.[5]

In a direct-measurement study, Jourard found that physical contact and verbal self-disclosures by an experimenter elicited more self-disclosures from subjects than did a more neutral, nontouching stance.[6] One assumes that the experimenter conveyed a feeling of warmth and personal interest.

The validity of questionnaire studies of self-disclosure is questionable. One's own impressions of one's actions are frequently at variance with actual performance. The most widely used and validated questionnaire, the Jourard Self-Disclosure Questionnaire, was found *not* to correlate with objective measures of self-disclosure by Hurley and Hurley.[7]

Self-disclosure is a multifaceted phenomenon. Self-disclosingness is a personality variable. It is also influenced by interpersonal context. In social settings, self-disclosingness is partially determined by the willingness of others to risk openness. The same was found true in the laboratory.

While the studies reported above suggest that disclosures of warm feelings enhance openness, Sullivan has reported a study in which "gripey" simulated cohorts elicited more disclosures from an experimental group of student nurses than did pleasant, cheerful simulated cohorts.[8] It is tempting to speculate that the students had more to complain about than to be pleasant about and were more comfortable complaining to others who also appeared dissatisfied.

Encounter Group Research

Encounter group research sheds more light on disclosingness by the leader and on the effects of his disclosures. Encounter groups are described as a group experience for emotionally sound persons, to help them become more aware of their potential for living and enjoying life through emotional encounter with others.

Lieberman, Yalom, and Miles made an extensive, controlled study of eighteen encounter groups organized on the Stanford University campus as an elective undergraduate course for which academic credit was given.[9] Of the eighteen groups, sixteen were led by experienced leaders, each outstanding in his own approach. There was a great diversity of theoretical orientation among the group leaders, but leader behavior seemed more related to the leader's personality than his theoretical orientation. Two of the groups were led by tape-recorded instructions.

Each group lasted thirty hours, with a highly variable clustering of hours. Some groups met for ninety minutes twice a week. Others had only a few lengthy sessions. Data were obtained prior to the group sessions, a week or two afterward, and six to eight months after completion of the group experience. Data about the students came from individual interviews, interviews of friends, and observations made by recorders at the group sessions and by the students in the group. Changes in students were rated in terms of (1) his values, (2) his attitude toward encounter-type experiences, (3) his ability to cope with problems and relationships, (4) his self-view, including self-esteem, self-image, and the degree of agreement between his self-image and his ideal self, and (5) his view of others as harsh or lenient, simple or complex, and of his opportunities for friendship as limited or open.

Four basic aspects of leader behavior formed the basis of six leader types, which strongly correlated with outcome. The four aspects of leader behavior were Emotional Stimulation, Caring, Meaning Attribution, and Executive Function.

An Emotionally Stimulating leader emphasized intrusive modeling and use of self. He challenged and confronted the group, revealed his feelings, personal values, attitudes, and beliefs. He frequently participated as a member, exhorted the group and drew attention to himself.

A Caring leader protected group members from each other and offered friendship, love, warmth, genuineness, and acceptance. He expressed real concern for other persons in the group.

High-Meaning Attribution is ascribed to leaders who provided concepts as a basis for understanding, interpretation, and a framework for changing one's self.

Executive Functioning by leaders is defined as limit, rule, and goal setting, managing time, pacing, stopping, blocking, and interceding. Specific behaviors and emotional release were prescribed rather than demonstrated.

The most effective leaders were rated as moderate in Stimulation, high in Caring, users of Meaning Attribution, and moderate in Executive Function. Less effective leaders were either very low or very high in Stimulation, low in Caring, low in Meaning Attribution, and very high or very low in Executive Behavior. High Caring in the absence of Meaning Attribution was of little value.

The four basic aspects of leader behavior were developed into an empirical typology of leaders with six categories: *energizers, providers, social engineers, impersonals, laissez-faires,* and *managers.* Energizers gave intense Emotional Stimulation and moderate to high Caring and Executive Function. Providers were high in Caring and Meaning Attribution and made moderate use of Emotional Stimulation and Executive Function. Social Engineers used group-oriented Meaning Attribution with moderate Caring, low Emotional Stimulation, and variable degrees of Executive Function. Impersonals were moderately high in Emotional Stimulation and low in Caring and Executive Function. Laissez-faires used moderate to high Emotional Stimulation and were low in the other three areas. Managers were extremely high in the Executive dimension.

Individuals whose psychological functioning was impaired by the group experience were defined as casualties. Providers produced the most positive changes and had few negative outcomes. Tape groups had no casualties. Energizers and impersonals conducted groups with high casualty rates. When the students who profited most were interviewed, they did not attribute their gains to the behavior of the leader.

Student casualties reported that the behavior of the leader had strongly affected them, especially when the students had high expectations of the group, few coping skills, and little support or direction from the group leader. Leaders of the groups with the most casualties behaved in highly idiosyncratic ways, unrelated to the needs of the group. The most destructive group leader jumped on a male group member, after having said, "You turn me on," hugged him for a few minutes, and kissed him on the cheek. He then said he had been "turned on" to homosexuality while interacting with his sons.

These studies demonstrate that self-disclosingness and genuineness per se are of less value than *what* is exposed of the leader, the *context* in which it is exposed, and the *style* of disclosure. Uses of self that belittled, alienated, or confused were destructive. Statements of concern and positive involvement with the students had a generally positive effect, but in order to be effective, the therapist first needed to provide a cognitive framework.

Studies from Psychotherapy

Studies of psychotherapy are difficult to assess. Many researchers, especially group therapists, do not distinguish between psychotherapy groups and short-term interactional groups composed of volunteers. There is a vast difference in context for therapist and patient in these two situations. A person willing to identify himself as a patient seeking professional help is ordinarily strongly motivated to self-disclose, unless he is blocked by unawareness of his feelings or by emotional reactions to himself or his therapist. Individuals who suffer emotional difficulties but are unwilling to seek formal therapy may attend brief quasi-therapy groups. Their motivation to disclose is minimal. They cling to their primary identification as student volunteers or paid participants and can readily rationalize their resistance as a wish to be treated on an egalitarian basis rather than as patients.

Many of the research studies are complicated by the naiveté of the therapists who are often graduate students with little experience. They do not realize they are working with unmotivated patients, and they do not have adequate professional skills to facilitate cooperation. The untrained therapist resorts to ordinary social means for promoting mutual disclosure; he discloses himself, hoping that others will follow his lead. Group members follow his lead—not in the expectation of dealing with significant emotional problems but to help complete the experiment—to win the approval and avoid the disapproval of the leader and the other group members. Data from therapy conducted by inexperienced persons on unmotivated subjects are not comparable to data from the treatment of motivated patients by experienced professionals, but they must be mentioned because they are the basis for much of the argument in favor of self-disclosure by the therapist.

Effects on Patient Disclosure

My own studies of self-disclosingness by group therapists do not support the findings with experimental subjects that disclosure begets disclosure. In collaboration with Frank Cody and Barry Rosson, I studied four short-term psychotherapy groups. We attempted, with only a moderate degree of success, to govern our levels of self-disclosure and measure the effects of our disclosingness on the disclosingness of our patients.[10] The degree to which we were able to vary our self-disclosure was limited by situational and unconscious intrapsychic factors. We hypothesized that disclosure of feelings by therapists would stimulate disclosure of feelings by patients. To test our hypothesis, we attempted to convey here-and-now feelings in two groups and to be neutral in the other two. We disclosed here-and-now feelings because they lend themselves well to quantification and because this technique has been endorsed in group psychotherapy literature as an effective therapeutic technique.

We analyzed fifteen-minute videotaped segments of each session and scored statements which followed the general formula as statements of here-and-now feelings.

| I | (feel) | (sad) | (with) | you, or |
| I | (am feeling) | (happy) | (toward) | you. |

The specific criteria which led to this formula were:

1. *A statement which requires no inference.* We required a direct statement of feeling. Statements such as, "I'm sorry," "I feel apologetic," or "I feel defensive," were rejected because they only hinted at underlying guilt, remorse, or a sense of having to defend against an undefined feeling in one's self.
2. *A statement for which the patient assumes responsibility.* We required the person who declared a feeling to assume responsibility for it, by saying, "*I* am sad," or "*I* feel afraid."
3. *A statement which is affective rather than cognitive* We did not score, "I am surprised," or "I am confused," because they are not statements of here-and-now feelings.
4. *A statement about a situation within the group which involves the patient here and now.* We scored sentences when they referred to events in the same group session. We did not score a psychological diagnosis such as, "I am an angry person."

We did not score answers to direct questions which did not include a statement of feeling. For example:

Q. "Are you angry?"
A. "Yeah, a little bit."
Q. "Whom do you like better of the two girls?"
A. "Betsy."

We excluded statements that were essentially negations of feelings, such as, "I don't feel angry," or, "I don't feel uncomfortable," although we did score the phrase, "I don't like . . . ," because it states dislike.

The psychotherapeutic technique in these studies was highly confronting and placed great value on the expression of here-and-now feelings. We attempted during each patient's first group session to establish a limited therapeutic goal that had some likelihood of success. For example, we contracted with one woman to reduce her guilt about her emotional need for her nine-year-old daughter, the only one of her five children she was unable to give into the custody of her ex-husband.

Analysis of the data revealed no correlation between the number of here-and-now affective self-disclosures by the patients and the number of here-and-now affective self-disclosures by the cotherapists.

Kangas has reported two studies in which he finds that self-disclosingness by the leader correlates with self-disclosure by group members. In his first study, he and another graduate student each conducted two groups for four fifty-minute sessions. The group members were undergraduate volunteers. Group members disclosed more (r = 0.72) to the more disclosing leader. No other possible facilitating factor, such as greater professional experience or better rapport, was investigated. In a subsequent study, he contrasted the effects of self-disclosure by the leader on three different groups: an adolescent therapy group that met for six months, a traditional therapy group of six student volunteers that met an hour a week for ten weeks, and a marathon therapy group of six student volunteers that met for one ten-hour session. There was strong correlation between leader and group member self-disclosure in the traditional and marathon groups; however, a negative correlation existed between leader and group member disclosure in the adolescent therapy group, the only group organized for therapy per se.[11]

Otstott and Scrutchins performed the only study comparing the efficacy of therapist self-disclosure with other techniques of facilitating patient disclosure. They examined therapist-patient interactions in an ongoing leader-centered therapy group conducted by an experienced psychologist. They scored fifteen- to thirty-minute interactions between the leader and five patients for significant self-disclosure. Five categories of therapist intervention were scored: open invitation to talk, interpretation, confrontation, verbal follow, and self-disclosure. Open invitation to talk and confrontation were by far the most effective means of promoting disclosure by the patients.[12]

OUTCOME STUDIES

Truax and Carkhuff measured the relationship between therapist transparency (congruence or genuineness) and patient disclosure in 306 samples from the individual therapy of sixteen hospitalized patients who were in treatment up to three and a half years. They found that the greater the therapist's transparency, the greater the patient's self-exploration.[13]

Truax and Carkhuff also sampled every fifth interview throughout the therapy of fourteen hospitalized schizophrenic patients who were seen by different therapists (no therapist saw more than two patients) in treatment lasting from six months to three and a half years. When raters judged the samples for patient self-exploration (disclosure) and compared the ratings with several measures of clinical improvement, they found a positive correlation. Based on these two studies, Truax and

Carkhuff concluded that greater therapist disclosure produces greater self-exploration by patients, which in turn leads to greater clinical improvement. However, for a population of forty institutionalized delinquents in group therapy, the opposite was true. The more-disclosing delinquents improved the least.[14]

Truax's scale of therapist transparency, by which the openness of the therapist was measured, is actually a measure of obvious manipulation. At the zero point, "there is explicit evidence of a very considerable discrepancy between the therapist's experiencing and his current verbalization . . . the therapist or counselor makes striking contradictions in his statements . . . or, the therapist may contradict content with voice quality." At the highest level, "there is an openness to experiences and feeling by the therapist of all types—both pleasant and hurtful—without traces of defensiveness or retreat into professionalism . . ."[15] A more appropriate zero point is a consistent, nonmanipulative, neutral attitude. Flagrant manipulation and misrepresentation have no place in psychotherapy. What Truax and Carkhuff demonstrate is that patients respond poorly to insincerity and manipulation.

Strassberg and colleagues investigated self-disclosure by the therapist in group psychotherapy. They studied 18 chronic schizophrenic inpatients whose average length of hospitalization was ten years. Greater disclosure by the therapist was associated with higher levels of patient disclosure, but patients who were more revealing showed less improvement over the ten-week course of treatment (three one-hour sessions per week) than did those who were less revealing.[16]

Barrett-Lennard studied forty-two clients treated by twenty-one counselors of varying degrees of sophistication. He measured "the counselor's psychological availability or willingness to be known," utilizing a questionnaire administered to clients that contained items such as the following: "He will freely tell me his own thoughts and feelings when I want to know them." "He is uncomfortable when I ask him something about himself." "He is unwilling to tell me how he feels about me."

Barrett-Lennard found that the more experienced of his group of therapists were less "willing to be known" than the less experienced therapists. Willingness to be known on the part of the therapist showed no significant association with successful outcome of therapy.[17]

Whitehorn and Betz suggest that the degree of openness of the therapist is less significant than what he discloses to the patient. They found that schizophrenic patients treated by psychiatrists in training improved most when they were approached in an active, personal way. Techniques of passive permissiveness or efforts to develop insight by interpretation had much less therapeutic value. The active therapists revealed their interest in their patients as persons and their willingness to be involved with them. The passively permissive therapists revealed their disinterest and their fears of involvement, or unwillingness to be involved as people, with the patients.[18]

Summary

The common-sense idea that disclosure begets disclosure is supported by questionnaire studies and by direct observation of persons in laboratory, work, and social settings.

A different picture emerges in the psychotherapist-patient relationship. Unfortunately, much of the research in this area is naive and based on studies of quasi-patients in pseudotherapy. The data suggest that self-disclosingness per se does not consistently augment patient disclosure. Neither high therapist disclosure nor high patient disclosure consistently correlates with improvement in psychotherapy.

Lieberman's monumental study of encounter groups and Whitehorn and Betz's study of schizophrenic patients strongly suggest that the crucial factors in therapeutic outcome are not how much the therapist's real self is exposed or the amount of information the therapist discloses about himself. Rather, they are: *what* is disclosed, *how* it is disclosed, and *in what context* it is disclosed. As Meltzoff and Kornreich suggest, there is more to the therapeutic relationship than the therapist-offered conditions.[19] We must also consider the nature of the patient's emotional difficulty and the circumstances under which we are attempting to deal with it.

References

1. Jourard, S. M. and Resnick, J. L.: Some effects of self-disclosure among college women. *J. Humanist. Psychol.* 10:84–93, 1970.

2. Drag, L. R.: Experimenter—subject interaction: A situational determinant of differential levels of self-disclosure. Unpublished Master's thesis, University of Florida, 1968.

3. Powell, W. J.: Differential effectiveness of interviewers' interventions in an experimental interview. *J. Counsel. Psychol.* 32:210–215, 1968.

4. Jourard, S. M.: Self-disclosure and other cathexis. *J. Abnorm. Soc. Psychol.* 59:428–431, 1959.

5. Shapiro, J. G., Krause, and Truax, C. B.: Therapeutic conditions and disclosure beyond the therapeutic encounter. *J. Counsel. Psychol.* 16:290–294, 1969.

6. Jourard, S. M.: *Self-Disclosure: An Experimental Analysis of the Transparent Self.* Wiley-Interscience, New York, 1971.

7. Hurley, J. R., and Hurley, S. J.: Toward authenticity in measuring self-disclosure. *J. Counsel. Psychol.* 16:271–274, 1969.

8. Sullivan, J. D.. Self-disclosure: measurement, relation with other personality dimensions and modifiability. Unpublished doctoral dissertation, Division of Psychology, The University of Texas Health Science Center at Dallas, 1971.

9. Lieberman, M. A., Yalom, I. D. and Miles, M. B.: *Encounter Groups: First Facts.* Basic Books, New York, 1973.

10. Weiner, M. F., Cody, V. F., and Rosson, B.: Studies of therapist and patient affective self-disclosure. *Group Process* 6:27–42, 1974.

11. Kangas, J. A.: Group members' self-disclosure: a function of preceding self-disclosure by leader or other group member. *Comp. Group Studies,* February, 1971, pp. 65–70.

12. Otstott, R. I., and Scrutchins, M. P.: Therapist behaviors preceding high degrees of client self-disclosure. Unpublished Master's thesis, University of Texas at Arlington, 1974.

13. Truax, C. B., and Carkhuff, R. R.: Client and therapist transparency in the psychotherapeutic encounter. *J. Counsel. Psychol.* 12:3–9, 1965.

14. Ibid.

15. Truax, C. B., and Mitchell, K. M.: Research in certain interpersonal skills in relation to process and outcome. In *Handbook of Psychotherapy and Behavior Change: An Empirical Analysis.* Bergen, A. E. and Garfield, S. L., eds. Wiley, New York, 1971.

16. Strassberg, D. S., Roback, H. B., Anchor, K. N., and Abramowitz, S. I.: Self-disclosure in group therapy with schizophrenics. *Arch. Gen. Psychiatry* 32:1259–1261, 1975.

17. Barrett-Lennard, G. T.: Dimensions of therapist response as causal factors in therapy change. *Psychol. Monogr.* 76 (562), 1962.

18. Whitehorn, J. C., and Betz, B. J.: A study of psychotherapeutic relationship between physicians and schizophrenic patients. *Am. J. Psychiatry* 13:383–400, 1954.

19. Meltzoff, J., and Kornreich, M.: *Research in Psychotherapy.* Atherton, New York, 1970, p. 76.

5.

General Principles of Psychotherapeutic Intervention

This chapter sets the stage for consideration of self-disclosure by the therapist as a therapeutic medium and establishes a frame of reference by which self-disclosures can be evaluated. Much of the material presented is a review of the basic concepts that form the cornerstone for any type of psychotherapy: the elements of psychotherapy, the factors that govern the therapist's choice of intervention, levels of intervention, modes of intervention, and the personal needs of the therapist as they affect his relationship with patients.

Elements of Psychotherapy

A discussion of the basic elements of psychotherapy must be prefaced by consideration of transference and countertransference. Much of what the patient presents in psychotherapy is transference-determined. Transference is the patient's unconscious attempt to relive or master some aspect of his past life in the therapeutic hour. Instead of remembering the conflicts he has repressed, he acts them out in the therapeutic session. Initially useful in establishing a cooperative relationship and in determining where the patient's main conflicts lie, the transference becomes a resistance to self-awareness that must be dealt with.

Countertransference, strictly defined, is the therapist's unconscious attempt to relive or master some aspect of his own past life in the therapy hour with his patients, instead of consciously coming to grips with his conflicts. Countertransference is often defined more broadly as the total of the therapist's personal reactions to the patient. In this book, a strict definition of countertransference will be used. Those reactions of the therapist which stem directly from the patient's behavior or from the therapist's current personal needs will be described simply as the feelings of the therapist toward the patient.

Effective therapy demands an awareness of the operation of transference and countertransference in the patient-therapist relationship. Statements made about the therapist by patients are easily taken literally if close to the mark, even though they may be largely transference-based. An intervention calculated to meet a patient's need is often countertransference-based. Transference and countertransference-based behaviors are difficult to recognize. A patient, for example, may be correct in his appraisal of the therapist as bright and knowledgeable. He may also have a strong transference need to focus on this aspect of the therapist. Immediate disclosure by the therapist of facts confirming the patient's hypothesis about his intelligence and breadth of knowledge will serve to reinforce the transference as a resistance to exploration of other feelings about the therapist. The therapist's intense desire to disclose may be partly based on the patient's urgent need for the information, but it may also be the therapist's attempt to block awareness of his own unconscious mental processes. There are several useful means for identifying transference and countertransference. The urgency with which the therapist or patient is impelled to act on his feeling (therapist or patient) is an important clue. The greater the urgency felt, the more likely transference or countertransference is operative. In general, the greater the intensity of the feeling and the less it appears realistically related to the immediate patient-therapist interaction, the greater the possibility of transference or countertransference. The therapist's most effective means of detecting transference and countertransference is awareness of both parties' present-day relationships and interactions, especially as they play on known psychological vulnerabilities, and an awareness of the reactions of each to the significant persons in his past life. He can bring this knowledge into play if he can attain a modicum of detachment from the patient and if he allows himself time to reflect before acting or reacting. An awareness of the transference-countertransference dimension of treatment helps to predict and explain the variable usefulness of each element of psychotherapy at different times.

The most basic element in psychotherapy is cooperation: the patient's willingness to work within the framework provided by the therapist. Cooperation is based on a realistic hope and expectation of change and on a perception of the therapist as accepting and empathic.[1] Cooperation is also transference-based, the transference having its roots in positive relationships with important persons in one's early life. A much-abused person who has suffered rejection, abandonment, or exploitation by the important persons in his early life may be unable to trust sufficiently to cooperate. The issue of the development of trust in the therapeutic relationship will be dealt with in a later chapter. It will suffice for now to state that trust is not only necessary for cooperation but also for learning; the next ingredient is psychotherapy.

Learning is the core of psychotherapy.[2] Patients learn about themselves and about dealing more effectively with life's problems in many ways. The therapist can share information he has learned through his training or experiences. Feedback, or sharing with the patient what the therapist experiences in reaction to his behavior, is an important aspect of the learning process for many patients who are unaware of the impact of their behavior on others. Insight, another important aspect of learning, comes about as the result of working through resistances against awareness of unconscious mental processes.

Catharsis, the expression of formerly withheld or suppressed feelings, has long been recognized as an important avenue for the relief of emotional symptoms. Catharsis discharges overwhelming affects and may also involve a more primitive process by which undesirable elements taken into one's self are expelled.[3]

Identification plays an important role in psychotherapy. Initially, identification with the therapist's acceptance and inquiring attitude allows the patient to tolerate the deprivation necessary in the early stages of therapy. This identification, in addition to a positive transference, forms the early basis of the therapeutic alliance between patient and psychotherapist. Later, the patient begins to identify with the healthy aspect of the therapist, himself, and other persons and lessens his ties to the less adaptive aspects of his own personality.

Given a positive relationship, patients become able to follow constructive suggestions made by the therapist. This does not imply a slavish dependency, which in itself is a resistance to maturation, but does involve some wish to please an esteemed person, or at least a willingness to respect the therapist's knowledge. The trust implied in the patient's willingness to accept suggestions from the therapist in areas that are inaccessible to others' suggestions also implies the operation of transference factors, in addition to the reality-based trust that has developed in the course of the therapeutic relationship.

To maintain the changes the patient has achieved, he must be able to obtain support or reinforcement, not only from the therapist, but from others in his daily life. This support can be praise or mere acceptance of what the patient is now becoming. An environment hostile to change can negate the efforts of patient and therapist alike.

In the course of therapy aimed at ameliorating one's coping ability or one's self-understanding, patient and therapist alike must be willing to bear the tensions of confronting emotional issues. An important side effect of facing these issues is the development of the capacity to bear anxiety and the ability to reflect on what one does or contemplates doing.

No learning is useful unless it is applied to one's real life situation. This is the difference between intellectualization (intellectual insight), in which one merely rationalizes what one is, and emotional insight, which forms the basis for new behavior and new ways of thinking.

Finally, what has been learned can be effectively integrated only by continual reapplication of the newly learned patterns of thinking and behavior. From the standpoint of the therapist, this is the process of working through. He works to dispel the resistances that continue to crop up and to obstruct the effective utilization of what has been gained. From the standpoint of the patient, it is a continuous reminding of what he has learned and an ongoing confrontation of his attempts to evade what he already knows.

Any contemplated therapeutic intervention should contain one of the elements described above. If it contains none, the therapist owes himself and his patient a careful evaluation to be certain that the therapist's impulse is not irrelevant, or worse, antitherapeutic.

Factors Governing Choice of Intervention

The factors governing all psychotherapeutic interventions are the type of intervention, its dosage, and timing. I will explore only one type of intervention, self-disclosure, as a therapeutic medium. I will consider its dosage and timing in terms of six variables: the type and goal of therapy, the context of the therapist-patient relationship, the patient's ego strength, the psychological relationship between therapist and patient, the patient's feelings about the therapist, and the therapist's feelings about the patient. The examples that follow show the range of possibilities for self-disclosure but do not reflect the frequency with which therapists self-disclose. The average psychotherapist is relatively neutral. My own self-disclosures are relatively infrequent. They are at times more related to my own wish to relax and be a person in the relationship with my patient than to a specific therapeutic need of the patient.

TYPE AND GOAL OF THERAPY
Psychotherapies and psychotherapeutic interventions can be divided into three types, based on their approach to mental processes and to object need: *repressive, ego-supportive,* and *evocative.* Mental processes refer primarily to the unconscious aspects of one's thinking. Object need refers to one's need for real people in his life, independent of any specific neurotic structure or projection of infantile needs. Patients and therapists basically wish to regard each other as real people. However, certain therapeutic approaches are more effective when the therapist deliberately imposes a barrier that keeps him, as a person, out of the therapeutic interaction. Tarachow terms this the *therapeutic barrier.*[4]

Repressive
Repressive therapies are highly structured and aim to reinforce the repression of unconscious material. They utilize direct teaching, foster identification with the therapist's values, and focus on coping techniques that help deal with one's own feelings and interpersonal relationships and the development of interpersonal skills.[5] Regression is discouraged because of its potential for arousing material from the unconscious. Patients are encouraged to adopt slogans such as "think positively" or "move your muscles," which help them toward positive alternative behaviors. Repressive measures include reassurance that certain thoughts are normal. Their assets and basic health or goodness are stressed, and attention is diverted from the unconscious toward problems of daily living.

There are many repressive techniques in use today. A few of the more common approaches are Ellis' rational-emotive therapy, Glasser's reality therapy, the behavior modification techniques, biofeedback, and relaxation exercises. Undoubtedly, the most common repressive treatment administered by physicians is the use of tranquilizing or mood-elevating drugs in the context of a benign, authoritarian relationship.

A repressive approach is used with individuals who have little capacity, need, or motivation for insight. It is indicated for acute situational crises and for individuals of low ego strength whose daily functioning would be compromised by having to deal with unconscious material. The repressive style ordinarily makes use of the therapeutic barrier; the patient's vulnerability to his own object need would lead him into unsuccessful attempts to incorporate the therapist as a real person. Repressive measures are appropriate in the early stages of all types of psychotherapy. They facilitate cooperation with the treatment and minimize anxiety until a bond is established between patient and therapist. Repressive measures are also appropriate in ego-supportive and evocative therapies when the patient's anxiety becomes so intense that it works against the treatment process.

Ego-Supportive

Most once-a-week therapies operate on an ego-supportive level, the treatment approach in which therapists are most likely to lower their therapeutic barrier. Its focus is interpersonal. Ego-supportive therapy is indicated for a patient who has greater capacity and motivation for self-understanding than a person for whom a repressive approach is indicated. The candidate for ego-supportive therapy is able to manage his own life, while the candidate for repressive therapy may need hospitalization or medication, in addition to his psychotherapy, to bolster his ego functioning.

Ego-supportive therapies require less structure than repressive therapies. The ego-supportive therapies encourage use of repression in areas the ego cannot otherwise handle and the development of less crippling ego defenses. The therapist confronts patients with their denial, projection, and rationalization. They are encouraged to take responsibility for their feelings but are not encouraged to explore the unconscious roots of their feelings or perceptions. Perceptual distortions are corrected in the here and now. Regression is discouraged. The patient is encouraged to think for himself and to become aware of his behavior toward others and his reactions to the behavior of others.

Two of the basic mechanisms of ego-supportive therapy are *feedback* and *identification*. Feedback confronts the patient with the therapist's reactions to him, heightening the patient's awareness of his impact on others. Since the patient is not greatly regressed when he enters treatment and is not encouraged to regress during the treatment, it is easy for the therapist to deal with him as a real person. As a consequence, ego-supportive therapy is often very gratifying to patient and therapist alike. Each has a new potential friend with whom he can expand his sphere of positive relationships.

An in-depth exploration of the role of identification in therapy would require a discussion beyond the scope of this book, but a brief digression is in order.

Bandura postulates that one learns complex social behaviors primarily by imitating the behaviors and patterns of thinking modeled by highly valued persons.[6] Bandura's observations coincide with those of Anna Freud: children take into themselves highly feared or admired qualities of the persons in their environment they most strongly love or fear.[7] Identification is particularly useful in defending against external threat. Children, by taking on some aspect of a dreaded person or situation, convert anxious dread into pleasurable security.

One can identify with some physical aspect of a feared person, with his aggression (by becoming aggressive) or with his role. This "identification with the aggressor" is an important step in superego formation. Identification also reduces regression during adolescence as the child detaches from his parents and tries to avoid becoming completely self-absorbed by attaching himself to peers, not as adults make friends, maintaining their own individuality, but through identification: dressing alike, acting alike, etc.

Kohut has given an account of the identification process in the training analysis of analytic candidates with "narcissistic" personality organizations."[8] At first, the "narcissistic" analysand does not seem to react emotionally to his analyst. For example, there is no reaction to interruptions of treatment. Later, the analysand reacts to interruptions in therapy by gross, unassimilated identifications with single features of the analyst. He may feel drawn to purchase an item of clothing identical to his analyst's during the latter's vacation. After repeated working through of similar events, identifications become less gross and indiscriminate. They become selective and focus on features and qualities that are compatible with and enhance the personality and talents of the analysand. These compatible, favorable qualities and skills of the analyst become more assimilated and differ from transient identifications with the aggressor formed in response to painful experiences with the analyst. As the patient's emotional investment in the analyst changes, he makes the pleasant discovery that he has acquired solid nuclei of autonomous functions in his family and professional life.

I doubt seriously that the above-discussed series of steps in identification is confined to the narcissistic personality. It is identical to the development of psychiatric residents who first emulate one supervisor, then another, until a blend is established that is compatible with their own personalities and interests.

I have treated several patients with an analytically oriented technique aimed at insight into unconscious dynamics only to find that, for these individuals, attempts at developing insight merely obstructed a more important process: identification with some aspect of me. Individuals for whom identification is one of the important therapeutic vehicles fall in all diagnostic categories. The importance of identification in the treatment does not correlate well with ego strength, but ego strength may relate to the aspect of the therapist with which the patient identifies. A marginally coping individual might identify with the therapist's positive outlook on life and become less gloomy. A better-integrated patient might make a professional identification and even change careers.

Some degree of identification with the therapist is necessary for the eventual individuation of the patient and his separation from the therapist. It is more important for some patients than others, based perhaps on the unavailability of suitable objects for identification in the patient's past or an impairment of the patient's ability to make the necessary identification at the appropriate point in psychosexual development.

For some patients, the process of identification fails to go beyond introjection. In my experience these are orally fixed individuals, usually nonpsychotic, who say they can feel my presence with them when they are alone, often have long conversations with me in fantasy, and find the introjected me to be more understanding than the real me. I have obviously been introjected as an idealized object but in this way provide considerable relief for some individuals.

Evocative

Evocative approaches stimulate emergence of material from the unconscious. Psychoanalysis is the prototype of one kind of evocative therapy. Psychoanalysis stimulates partial ego regression through an unstructured therapy hour, a lack of interpersonal cues, free association, and frustration of the patient's object needs. The ego regression results in a transference neurosis, in which the patient experiences his basic instinctual drives, his infantile conflicts, and his fixations as though they were part of his current interaction with the therapist.[9] He then attempts to rework his defenses against his instinctual drives to resolve his infantile conflicts and to overcome his fixations. This type of approach requires a stable life adjustment, intact reality testing, and a capacity for a nondestructive partial ego regression.

The patient must be able to reverse his ego regression at the end of each session and become aware of his feelings rather than act them out. Self-observation comes about through a "split" of the ego, one side caught up in the transference, the other observing itself in the transference relationship. The ego must also have sufficient strength to cope with the superego, so that it can observe its own defensive operations objectively rather than become self-accusatory.

An analytically oriented method requires that the therapist be able to frustrate his own, as well as the patient's, object needs. After their initial encounter, patient and therapist separate as people. It is the initial contact with the therapist and partial identification with him that makes the frustration bearable. Obviously, there are points in the therapeutic process when the therapist must relent to assure the patient that he is working with a real person.

Object relations exist only because the child and his mother cannot remain fused. Everyone, whether normal or neurotic, seeks to return to this period of symbiotic bliss through identification and object relations. Mature ego differentiation occurs only out of perceived necessity. The patient relinquishes his hold on the therapist as a real person so that he can learn more about himself. Each time the therapist treats the patient as a real person (loaning him fifty cents for parking), he temporarily assuages his interpersonal loneliness and, ultimately, his feelings of abandonment by his original symbiotic objects. A paradox in human development is that object relations, which we deem a mark of maturity, exist to circumvent the painful recognition of separateness.

Analytically oriented therapies are, in a sense, a process of deprivation. The patient is deprived of infantile gratification through interpretation ("it looks like you're trying to make me into an all-giving mother") to free the patient to pursue adult gratification. Viewed from this perspective, *every interpretation is a deprivation.*[10]

The psychoanalytic model is generally not suitable for therapists who need patients to regard them as real individuals, but this does not imply that the analytically based therapist is always neutral. The reality of the therapist is an important factor in maintaining ongoing therapy. At times, it is necessary for the therapist to introduce some aspect of himself not only as a tension-breaker but also to correct the patient's fantasies and distortions.[11]

Many active evocative techniques have been developed. Each

awaits the test of time. These techniques aim to rapidly break through the ego's defenses, to speed up and deepen the therapeutic process. They include gestalt therapy,[12] primal therapy,[13] and scream therapy.[14] In each of these approaches, the therapist actively prescribes verbal and nonverbal exercises designed to elicit repressed thoughts and feelings.

Evocative techniques have no place in the treatment of individuals with markedly impaired reality testing or impulse control, except under controlled circumstances in an institution. Evocative methods are also inappropriate for most adolescent patients, for whom additional regression threatens an already shaky ego.

THE REAL THERAPIST-PATIENT RELATIONSHIP

The real (nontransference) patient-therapist relationship refers to the context of their initial contact, the purpose of their relationship, and their working conditions. Two issues concerning the context of the initial patient-therapist contact are who has the problem and to what degree the patient is motivated to deal with the problem. When a patient is referred because his behavior troubles others but does not trouble him, the therapist must decide whether to point out the problem to the patient or to communicate information about the patient to the referring individual(s) so that they can better cope with him. In either course of action, the therapist must state whom he serves and in what capacity. If patient and therapist agree that the therapist's primary alliance is to the patient, they must agree on the aspect of the patient with which the therapist will ally himself.

It is necessary to establish how much the therapist will act on his own judgment of what is best for the patient. This includes the degree to which the therapist will actively interfere with, or attempt to manage, the patient's life, as well as the degree of confidentiality of the relationship. With outpatients, these issues are usually dealt with implicitly. When the patient requires hospitalization or has borderline coping ability, they are made explicit. These are not personal disclosures but statements of one's professional role in relation to the patient's needs. It is possible to take a further step toward building a relationship if the therapist states what he wishes he might do for the patient or how he reacts as a person to the patient. To a patient struggling against the idea of hospitalization, the therapist can say, "I respect and admire your wish to take care of yourself and manage your own affairs. On the other hand, I'm a bit scared at the difficulty you're having handling your urges to hurt yourself. I'd like to work with you as an outpatient, but to be on the safe side, I feel you should be hospitalized."

If a patient does not accept a problem as his own, the therapist must decide whether or not to maintain the treatment relationship until the patient acknowledges his problem. It is tempting to offer some aspect of one's self as a temporary link until the patient is willing to turn away from the therapist's personality to look at his own problems. The therapist can offer his interest, empathic concern, or part of his own life in building a personal connection with the patient. A therapist can tell stories about himself to child patients to help the child see that he is not in the usual coercive adult-child relationship, involving dominance and submission, but in a sharing partnership.

It is useful to help the patient distinguish between the therapist's role and his personality when they appear contradictory. A patient may equate his therapist's cheerful, outgoing personality with permissiveness or his self-restrained, serious demeanor with a wish to restrain the patient. One can make open statements about one's role to avoid unnecessary confusion of this sort, but most therapists allow patients to develop their own expectations and then work out the discrepancies in the treatment process. The therapist must be aware of the expectations his personality ordinarily stimulates in his patients so that he can distinguish between transference-based expectations and expectations based on reasonable observation. He must also be aware that correct observations by the patient can be largely transference-based.

THE PATIENT'S EGO STRENGTH

Before attempting to impart information to a patient, one must assess the patient's ego strength (his capacity for coping with reality and his own thoughts and feelings). Ego strength also involves the ability to distinguish observations from fantasy, feelings from fact. All of these factors influence one's capacity to receive and constructively integrate new information.

There is no direct correlation between the patient's ego strength and his wish for the therapist to act as a real person. Well-integrated patients are likely to voice anger and disappointment when a therapist who has been "real" assumes a more neutral stance. Less well-integrated patients may interpret and react to a shift toward neutrality as abandonment. Increased openness with the well-integrated patient may enhance a sense of camaraderie. Poorly integrated patients, uncertain of their ego boundaries, may experience fear that they will become engulfed by the therapist.

The relationship between self-disclosure by the therapist and the ego-strength of his patient is multifaceted. The less the patient's ego strength, the greater his need to experience his environment as it really is, rather than as a projection of his own fears and wishes. However, the patient who has little ego strength is very likely to misinterpret the therapist's disclosures or be unable to constructively integrate them into his thinking. For example, a female patient's wish for, and fear of, her therapist's sexual interest may increase when she learns her therapist has been recently divorced. This may intensify a psychotic regression. Suitable disclosures to patients of low ego strength enhance reality testing, reinforce impulse control, reduce fantasy, and augment the ego's defenses against disruptive aspects of the unconscious, whether the urge striving for expression is a murderous wish or a drive for closeness.

Although the patient with more ego strength has less need to experience the therapist as a real person, he is also less likely to be damaged by the therapist's disclosures. If the disclosures stimulate fantasy or intensify unconscious impulses, the therapist may note a strengthening of resistances, which signals the therapist to assume a more neutral stance until the consequences of the disclosure are worked through. A well-integrated patient is not directly damaged by a disclosure. The damage is to the therapeutic relationship, undermining its effectiveness by changing the focus from patient to therapist and by placing the object needs of the therapist above the treatment needs of the patient.

THE NATURE OF THE ALLIANCE

Interventions by the therapist may be therapeutic, nontherapeutic (that is, have no effect on therapy), or antitherapeutic. So may be the alliance between therapist and patient. Ideally, this contact occurs between the rational, health-seeking part of the patient and the rational, objectively observing aspect of the therapist. Other types of alliance are possible. Some patients hope to continue acting on their impulses rather than dealing with them and therefore seek out incompetent therapists. Patients who wish to reinforce the harsh aspects of their own consciences may seek a punitive, judgmental therapist. Those who wish to enhance their intellectual defenses may seek out therapists who promote rationalization, "explaining" behavior as the result of childhood traumas without confronting the patient with his present-day responsibility for changing this behavior.

Every patient is faced with the problem of trust. Can he trust his therapist to maintain confidences? Can he trust the therapist's expertise? The therapist must decide to what lengths he should go to convince the patient of his trustworthiness in these respects. Active attempts by the therapist to cultivate trust are seldom helpful. Disclosure by the therapist of his past successes or his good will toward the patient have little influence on the development of trust. The patient may choose to trust based on transference expectations or the therapist's reputation, or he may choose to await evidence of trustworthiness before investing himself in the therapist or the therapeutic process. In the course of their regular contact, the patient observes and experiences his therapist's self-awareness, his self-confidence, and his capacity for understanding—giving necessary permissions and setting necessary limits. The patient then decides whether his therapist merits trust. Exaggerated trust or mistrust point to the operation of transference factors, which may need to be resolved. One should not attempt to manipulate the patient into a more objective view of oneself by talking about one's shortcomings to reduce overvaluation or, if undervalued, one's accomplishments. It is reasonable, however, to confront the patient with obvious aspects of the therapist that he ignores because of transference needs or wishes.

The object need of therapist and patient affects the alliance. Therapists with strong object needs tend to repel schizoid individuals, who feel drained by human contact. A masochistic, self-sacrificing patient may be attracted by his therapist's need for recognition, but this type of alliance may perpetuate his psychopathology. Patients with great object need may be seen as "too draining" by some therapists. Other therapists see the possibility of mutual gratification during the course of therapy and do effective psychotherapy in a relationship that involves patient and therapist being personally open with one another.

THE PATIENT'S FEELINGS ABOUT THE THERAPIST

In disclosing himself to a patient, the therapist must take into account the patient's feelings toward him. This includes the patient's probable unconscious feelings, as well as his consciously experienced and expressed feelings. Every patient has some transference feelings. Other feelings stem from the real situation—anger, for example, if the therapist forgets his appointment or keeps him waiting inordinate lengths of time. Still other feelings are based on nontransference expectations, such as the reasonable assumption that the patient will find some degree of acceptance by the therapist.

In general, disclosures made to a patient who feels positively about the therapist will enhance his positive feelings. If the patient has strongly negative feelings, they will tend to be reinforced. It is when the patient is not experiencing an extreme of positive or negative feelings toward the therapist that self-disclosures are most useful as information and least prejudicial to the therapeutic relationship. At these points, the therapist can introduce information about himself to correct transference distortions and to help the patient understand what he can realistically expect from his therapist.

The therapist can manipulate his patients' feelings through self-disclosure. However, one cannot accurately predict the outcome. The same disclosure, made to different persons who feel the same way about the therapist, may have very different effects. If the therapist reveals himself to be a warm, compassionate person, he may reinforce positive feelings in some patients; others, in spite of basically positive feelings, may suspect him to be a sentimental fool.

In repressive therapies, positive feelings toward the therapist are accepted as a matter of course and are not examined in the therapeutic relationship. The therapist attempts to dispel negative feelings toward himself by apologizing for, or explaining away behavior by which he has antagonized the patient. Negative transference feelings are also dealt with by explanation and rationalization. The therapist may reveal negative feelings of his own that developed under similar circumstances to promote the patient's identification with him and to indicate the essential normality of the patient's feelings.

Ego supportive therapies explore the current factors in the patient's reaction to the therapist. Since the patient in an ego-supportive therapy has enough ego strength to feel and express his negative feelings toward the therapist without disrupting their relationship or acting in a self-destructive way, awareness and expression of both positive and negative feelings are encouraged. The therapist stimulates his patient's expressions of feelings by sharing his own feelings, being careful that the focus does not shift away from the patient to the therapist.

In evocative therapies, the therapist considers dynamic and genetic factors as he explores the patient's feelings toward him. Self-disclosures are used to correct transference distortions only after the patient has fully experienced the transference feeling and has explored all of its ramifications. In repressive and ego-supportive therapies, the therapist begins to correct transference distortions early to prevent intensification to the point that therapy is obstructed. In an evocative therapy, the transference is allowed to become an obstruction and is then dealt with by an appropriate self-disclosure or interpretation.

If the therapist is seen as the most important supplier of the patient's object needs, he must be careful to withhold disclosures that will stimulate intensely negative feelings toward him. Such disclosures may precipitate a suicide attempt or withdrawal from treatment.

When the patient's object needs are well supplied outside the treatment relationship, there is a greater likelihood that the patient's negative feelings will be talked out, and not acted out, in the therapeutic situation. On the other hand, revealing information that heightens positive feelings toward the therapist may reinforce a patient's masochistic demands to be dominated.

THE THERAPIST'S FEELINGS ABOUT THE PATIENT

Every therapist develops feelings about his patients. Sometimes his feelings enable him to do better work; other times they are detrimental to the therapeutic relationship. If the therapist wishes to disclose his feelings to a patient, he must first examine his wish. If he is responding to the patient's urgings, he must question the patient's motivation (at least to himself) before replying. This is especially true when the therapist or the patient feels that the disclosure is urgent, but there are certain exceptions. Disclosure is at times urgently needed, as the following example shows.

Mr. C. had been in treatment with me for about a year. During this time, he exposed his genitals on several occasions while on his front porch. He was apprehended, tried, and sentenced to two years in jail. He saw me intermittently between the time he was apprehended and the time he was jailed.

The afternoon before he was to begin his jail sentence, he came to my office without an appointment and said he needed to see me. I saw him after office hours. He was quite agitated. He said he felt he had nothing to live for and that as far as he could see, his wife and I had deserted him. He said in a frightening way that he felt like killing himself and taking several others with him. Finally, he seemed to calm down and left the office. I was relieved. He had a history of impulsive, destructive behavior and was both bigger and stronger than I.

A few minutes later he returned with a wicked-looking instrument he called a pike. He told me that he was going to kill me. I was frightened, tremulous, and did not try to hide it. I told him that I did not want to die, both for my own sake and the sake of my family. I told him I was scared to death of him and pleaded for my life. He ultimately relented and handed the weapon over to me. We talked briefly. In our talk, he told me that if I had been indifferent or had showed no fear, he might well have killed me. He left his weapon with me and went to jail to serve his sentence the next day. My self-disclosure had saved my life.

It is difficult, even in retrospect, to understand how my self-disclosure deterred Mr. C. Perhaps it helped restore his sense of potency to know that he had held my life in his hands and had voluntarily relinquished his chance to kill me. Perhaps he felt in that moment that he and I had experienced a moment of real contact.

The therapist must also take into account his feelings about the patient before he discloses other information. He must be careful not to disclose information to belittle a patient whom he dislikes or to enhance himself in the eyes of a patient from whom he wishes positive input.

The therapist's unconscious feelings and reactions to his patients are of even greater importance than his conscious attitudes. These unconscious aspects of the therapist manifest indirectly. To effectively deal with his own reactions, the therapist must observe not only his patient but himself. Not all the therapist's unconscious reactions to the patient are countertransference. Often, the therapist is reacting to his anxiety about his own feelings or impulse control.

Early in the treatment of a woman who had several extramarital liaisons, the therapist told her flatly that he did not intend to become physically involved with her. By employing this form of psychological overkill, the therapist confirmed his patient's view of herself as a malignant, destructive person. When the therapist, who was reacting to his own anxiety, felt in better control of himself and felt the treatment was progressing satisfactorily, he told the woman that he was reacting to his own sexual feelings rather than a sexual provocation on her part. This greatly diminished her sense of "badness" and facilitated a fruitful exploration of her sexuality.

The therapist's object needs are a consideration in his disclosures to a patient. If a therapist wishes to disclose his need for the patient as a real person, he must determine if such a disclosure fits the treatment needs of his patient. The therapist can have real relationships with his patients only if no harm is done and some mutual good is accomplished. There are times the therapist's object needs will be great because of significant deprivation in his life. He must be sufficiently self-aware to know if he is impelled to be real to his patient by his object need, his countertransference, or by the patient's therapeutic need.

A repeated urge to self-disclose to particular patients suggests the operation of countertransference factors. The nature of the disclosure the therapist wishes to make can also give some clue to the nature of the countertransference. Disclosing sexual feelings toward a patient not only serves to confirm the patient's attractiveness but may also serve as a poorly sublimated seduction of the patient into a more sexualized relationship than he or she may require.

Levels of Intervention

The concept of "levels" of psychotherapeutic intervention is of great importance in the practice of psychotherapy. The "level" of the therapist's interventions helps shape the patient's conceptualization of his problems and provides a focus of investigation. The three most common points of focus are day-to-day reality, the emotional forces currently operating within the individual, and the relationship of a patient's past thoughts, feelings, and experiences to his present perceptions of, and his reactions to, his interpersonal and intrapsychic worlds. The levels of intervention that correspond to these three focal points can be designated as *here and now, dynamic,* and *genetic.*[15] Here-and-now interventions are appropriate in repressive, ego-supportive, and evocative therapies. Dynamic interventions are useful in supportive and evocative therapies. Genetic interventions are most effective in evocative therapies. My management of questions about my heart attack illustrates these three levels of intervention.

I felt it was more reasonable to let my patients know why I was suddenly unable to come to the office, where I was (those who wanted to know were told the name of the hospital), and when I was likely to return than to keep them guessing over such a long period of time. Not knowing any of the facts about my absence would have produced justifiable anger or fear that would have greatly complicated the treatment relationship and unnecessarily traumatized my patients. Having let them know, I was obliged to deal further with questions about my illness. I also dealt with their emotional reactions to my illness and my absence.

HERE AND NOW
A here-and-now intervention deals with the present, without reference to antecedents. For example, "I told you about my illness. I hope you will feel free to ask further questions if you are concerned." In this way, I recognized my patient as a concerned person and set a level of acceptable behavior in relation to questions about my health.

DYNAMIC
A dynamic intervention suggests psychological cause and effect. For example, "Did my comments about my heart attack affect the way you think about me or react to me?" Also, "How do you feel about my willingness to share information about my health with you?" Dynamic interventions lead to awareness of reactions to specific thoughts, feelings, and events, and help increase the patient's ability to observe himself objectively.

GENETIC
Genetic interventions deal with psychologically important historical events and are used with individuals who can constructively observe themselves. Bringing affective material from the past into the here and now permits emotional reworking of a feeling or thought pattern. The question, "Does my illness bring to mind anything from your own past?" invites rationalization if improperly timed. If raised at a time when guilt is easily mobilized, it may stimulate self-punishment.

Allowing a patient to become caught up in some aspect of the therapist's life can, on the other hand, block exploration of genetic material. After disclosing pertinent facts about himself, the therapist must be careful that the patient continues to be the subject of exploration.

Modes of Intervention

A therapist need not react openly to a patient's behavior. He may await further information so that his reaction will be founded on adequate data. Even if he has sufficient information, he may wait if the individual or group concerned is not currently able to deal with his reaction.

The therapist must be aware of his ordinary patterns of reaction to particular individuals and situations. When he does not react to behavior as he would ordinarily, he must determine what is different so that he can sort out countertransference reactions from reactions based on the patient's behavior and then decide on the most appropriate course.

My reactions to the patient are frequently a good indication of the type of psychopathology and pattern of interpersonal relationships with which I am dealing. When I find early in my relationship with a patient that I wish to jump to his defense and explain away his symptoms in terms of reality problems, I am usually responding to a profound ego regression and trying to help the patient externalize "the enemy" so that he will not attack himself. There is, of course, a countertransference element to this habitual reaction. So as to avoid acting on the countertransference aspect of my feelings, I often test the therapeutic validity of my reaction by suggesting overwhelming environmental stress as an etiologic factor. If the patient then begins to mobilize his resources to deal with the formerly unperceived stress, I know I am on the right track. If he continues to be wrapped up in self-accusation, I know that pursuing this approach serves to meet my countertransference needs and not the patient's therapeutic needs.

When I am angry with a patient, I find it useful to ask myself what I am responding to. Is it the patient's anger? Have I identified with this aspect of him? Am I reacting defensively to him? Is there, on the other hand, something in me seeking expression in the relationship? Before disclosing my reaction, it is often useful to ask the patient what he is feeling. If my own feeling is the result of an empathic identification, the patient has a chance to express himself directly and can experience the anger as originating within himself. If I disclose first, he is able to rationalize his anger as merely a response to my expression of anger.

There are at least four basic modes. of intervention: *acceptance, suppression, facilitation,* and *exploration.*

ACCEPTANCE

Acceptance is an empathic response. It implies understanding at an intuitive level and indicates that the message has some impact on the receiver. Acceptance does not imply evaluation of the material received. Acceptance is the acknowledgment that, at a given moment, one person has entered the world of another. It may be signaled by a nod of the head or, "I see." One may say, "I hear you," or "Oh!" The message is the same; it shows respect and recognizes the other person. If he feels he understands, the therapist can say, "I understand." If not, he can say, "I heard you, but I'm not sure I understand." Sharing one's self with a patient to demonstrate acceptance is not always wise, and should wait the development of an adequate therapeutic alliance.

Advocates of empathic responses by the therapist suggest that the therapist allow himself to experience and partake in the patient's irrationality, that he display his own feelings to demonstrate that he is with the patient, and that he force the patient to recognize him as a real person.[16] Whitehorn and Betz underscore the positive value of the therapist's ability to approach and deal with schizophrenic patients in an active, personal way.[17] The existential school goes further and recommends that the therapist become in some way as openly irrational as the patient, thus encouraging the patient to come out of himself and "meet" the therapist, thus changing his view of the world and himself.[18]

Empathy is an important part of the psychotherapist's armamentarium. It is based on the therapist's ability to partially identify with some important aspect of his patient. The information derived from this partial identification is used by the therapist to determine his subsequent interventions. Virtually no insight-oriented therapy can be conducted without this kind of empathic awareness.

Overt expression of empathy is quite another matter. It is, in a sense, exposure of the therapist's raw data, unrefined by his rational processes. A full exposition of the use of empathy requires inquiry into irrational psychotherapy, that is, the treatment of the irrational part of the patient by the irrational part of the therapist. Wolf and Schwartz deal with this subject extensively in a resounding condemnation of Whitaker's neoexistential point of view in which they state that it is the responsibility of the therapist, with rare and specifically indicated exceptions, to be rational in his relationship with his patient and to maintain a professional relationship.[19]

SUPPRESSION

Suppressive interventions aim to inhibit a thought, feeling, or act. They often involve the therapist's entering the patient's thoughts or life as a real person. Certain suppressive interventions are mandatory; one must directly suppress physical violence. The therapist may request reconsideration of a contemplated behavior, warn that the behavior will not be allowed, or physically restrain a patient.

When Miss. A., a young woman in group therapy, physically attacked another woman, the therapist jumped up and shouted that she must stop. When the same patient, a few sessions later, kicked over a table and started pounding on the floor and screaming, she was again ordered to stop. This was of no avail. When she began tearing down the draperies, the therapist physically restrained her and told her in no uncertain terms that she would be expelled from the group if she inflicted any further damage on the room or its occupants. The therapist made it clear that she was not going to be allowed to damage people or property.

In the presence of physical danger, safety takes precedence and dictates the form of intervention. In an evocative therapy, the therapist may wish to suppress other forms of activity, such as casual person-to-person conversation, after explaining to his patient that therapy progresses best if they stick to business.[20] In repressive or ego-supportive therapies, one may allow the tension release of social interchange to ease emotional pressures during the therapeutic session.

FACILITATION

Facilitative interventions bring material to awareness or make material available for discussion.

I had allowed Mrs. V., a patient in group psychotherapy, to postpone payment of her bill while she was in training on a new job. At the end of six months of nonpayment, she moved into a more expensive house and continued to maintain an expensive hobby. I told her that I was angry because she was taking advantage of my willingness to give her special treatment, putting her social ambitions and her pleasure ahead of her payment for therapy. We used this disclosure as a springboard to discuss the fact that she had been given special treatment by her father but had always suffered the subsequent anger of other family members who felt shortchanged.

Psychological facilitations range from a request that a patient talk to confrontation, clarification, and interpretation. A confrontation establishes that something is being avoided, for example, "I feel uncomfortable, as if something is different between us today. What do you feel?" A clarification aims to establish a sharp focus on a particular psychological event. One might say, "You have been talking abstractly about anger today. Maybe that's what I'm reacting to. Perhaps you're angry now." Confrontation and clarification refer not only to content but also to the direction of communication. For example, "I feel as if I'm a tape recorder when you look away while talking to me." Confrontation and clarification are utilized in repressive, ego-supportive, and evocative therapies.

Interpretation means "to make conscious the unconscious meaning, source, history, mode, or cause of a given psychic event," according to Greenson.[21] Interpretations, as stated earlier, embody little of the therapist as a person. However, the therapist may base his interpretation on a feeling reaction to the patient and disclose the feeling that led to it. Interpretation is usually reserved for the middle and end stages of ego-supportive and evocative treatment.

EXPLORATION

Explorative interventions help establish new links between thoughts, feelings, and behavior. In repressive therapies, one makes new links by suggesting alternatives to a given behavior. For example, if the question of how to stop smoking is raised by a patient, the therapist responds, "If I were you, I would chew gum each time I felt the urge to smoke a cigarette." Exploration of thoughts and behavior in terms of rational meaning is a valuable device in a supportive therapy, or when any therapy is at a supportive level. In dealing with a depressed patient who has had a nightmare, one might say, "In my experience, nightmares signify the resolution of a depression and give some clue to its origin." Thus, the therapist indicates that the nightmare is meaningful and that the patient can also come to understand its meaning. This answer also points toward the unconscious symbolism without involving primary process. In evocative therapies, one explores one's self through free association. The therapist can also stimulate self-exploration by encouraging the expression of fantasy.

The process of exploration may be inhibited by the entry of the therapist as a real person into the therapeutic process. By disclosing, the therapist promotes identification with himself. This may limit the patient's growth by saying, in effect, "I'm the therapist, and it's OK for me to be as I am. You, therefore, need not explore yourself further but accept yourself just as I do."

OTHER RESPONSES

The therapist must give concrete orienting information at the beginning of and at intervals during the course of any therapy. Ordinarily, less direct information is provided in an ego-supportive or evocative therapy than in a repressive therapy.

The therapist may also react with unplanned words or feelings. Crying in response to a patient's sadness or becoming angry when provoked are spontaneous, human responses on the part of the therapist and may result in therapeutic progress. When of reasonable degree, such reactions confirm that the therapist is human and that patients need not aspire to become superhuman. Spontaneity does carry with it, however, the risk of self-indulgence and must be tempered by the therapist's self-awareness and self-control.[22]

Meeting the Therapist's Needs

The therapist is entitled to meet some of his own needs in psychotherapeutic sessions. In meeting some of his own needs, he does not necessarily compromise his patient. A therapist can allow himself the gratification of recognition as a person by his patient, but he must not insist upon it. The patient who is interpersonally aware and relatively mature is often able to recognize the therapist as a person. On the other hand, many patients begrudge their therapist personal recognition; others are incapable of it. If withholding personal recognition from the therapist is a resolvable aspect of the patient's psychopathology, it needs to be explored. But with patients who would be compromised by having to acknowledge the therapist as a person, the issue of therapist recognition should not be pressed.

Events in the therapist's outside life, as well as in therapy sessions, affect his need to be recognized as a person by his patients. The more the therapist's object needs are frustrated in outside relationships, the more likely he is to press for real recognition by his patients. It may be detrimental to both patient and therapist if the therapist seeks gratification from his patients that is denied to him, or that he is unable to allow himself, in his life outside the office. This is in clear violation of the spirit of the therapeutic contract.

In allowing himself the gratification of being real with his patients, the therapist may be indirectly helpful by demonstrating that all persons have emotional needs and that the patient is not the empty, sucking parasite he feels himself to be.

Summary

In this chapter, I have dealt with the elements of psychotherapy, the factors which govern the dosage and timing of psychotherapeutic interventions, the levels of intervention, modes of intervention, and the question of meeting some of the therapist's needs in the treatment session.

Self-disclosures can serve virtually any type of therapeutic intervention, with the exception of an interpretation or an explorative intervention. In evaluating the potential usefulness of self-disclosure, one begins by exploring its transference and countertransference implications and by asking if it facilitates one of the nine therapeutic elements (cooperation, learning, catharsis, identification, suggestion, support, confronting emotional issues, application and integration of new learning). It must then be assessed in terms of the factors governing dosage and timing: the type and goal of treatment, the context of the therapeutic relationship, the patient's ego strength, the nature of the therapeutic alliance, and the feelings of patient and therapist about one another. Finally, there must be a selection of therapeutic level and of therapeutic mode, whether it be acceptance, suppression, facilitation, or exploration.

It is obvious that experienced therapists do not make such an extensive evaluation prior to each therapeutic intervention. The beginning therapist must. After considerable practice, the process becomes internalized and is carried out quickly at a preconscious level, much as the process of walking or throwing a baseball is relegated to lower motor centers instead of involving extensive decision making at a cortical level each time one takes a step or throws a ball.

The personal needs of therapists are also an important variable that has been largely overlooked in the literature on psychotherapy. In many cases, the therapist cannot and need not be incognito in the therapeutic relationship. Many patients who know much about their therapist as people are able to profit from psychotherapy. The greatest danger to therapist and patient lies in the insistence of the therapist that the patient meet the therapist's need for personal recognition, which amounts to an exploitative reversal of the implicit therapeutic contract.

References

1. Rogers, C. R.: The necessary and sufficient conditions of therapeutic personality change. *J. Consulting Psychol.* 22:95–103, 1957.

2. Strupp, H. H.: Toward a specification of teaching and learning in psychotherapy. *AMA Arch. Gen. Psychiatry* 21:203–212, 1969.

3. Weiner, M. F.: Catharsis, a review. *Group Process,* 7:173–184, 1977.

4. Tarachow, S.: *An Introduction to Psychotherapy.* International Universities Press, New York, 1963, p. 4.

5. Kadis, A., Krasner, J. D., Weiner, M. F., Winick, C., and Foulkes, S. H.: *Practicum of Group Psychotherapy.* Harper & Row, New York, 1974.

6. Bandura, A.: Psychotherapy based on modeling principles. In *Handbook of Psychotherapy and Behavior Change.* Bergin, A. E., and Garfield, S. L. eds. John Wiley, New York, 1971.

7. Freud, A.: *The Ego and the Mechanisms of Defense.* International Universities Press, New York, 1946.

8. Kohut, H.: *The Analysis of the Self,* International Universities Press, New York, 1971, pp. 161–167.

9. Greenson, R. R.: *The Technique and Practice of Psychoanalysis,* Vol. 1. International Universities Press, New York, 1967.

10. Tarachow, *op. cit.,* p. 13.

11. Greenson, *op. cit.*

12. Perls, F., Hefferline, R. F., and Goodman, P.: *Gestalt Therapy.* Julian Press, New York, 1951.

13. Janov, A.: *The Primal Scream.* Putnam, New York, 1970.

14. Casriel, D.: *A Scream Away from Happiness.* Gosset & Dunlap, New York, 1972.

15. Weiner, M. F.: Levels of intervention in group psychotherapy. *Group Process* 3:67–81, 1971.

16. Whitaker, C. A., and Malone, T. P.: *The Roots of Psychotherapy.* Blakiston, New York, 1953.

17. Whitehorn, J. C., and Betz, B.: A study of psychotherapeutic relationships between physicians and schizophrenic patients. *Am. J. Psychiatry* 3:321–331, 1954.

18. Havens, L. L.: The existential use of the self. *Am. J. Psychiatry* 131:1–10, 1973.

19. Wolf, A., and Schwartz, E. K.: Irrational psychotherapy, IV. *Am. J. Psychotherapy* 13:383–400, 1959.

20. Ormont, L.: Acting in and the therapeutic contract in group psychoanalysis. *Internat. J. Group Psychother.* 19:420–432, 1969.

21. Greenson, *op. cit.,* p. 39.

22. Weiner, M. F.: In defense of the therapist. *Psychosomatics* 10:156–158, 1969.

Part Two
Specific Indications
and Contraindications

6.

Indications for Use of Self

The degree of a therapist's disclosure to his patients tends to vary directly with their degree of interaction; the greater the interaction, the greater the disclosure. Generally, the active therapist reveals his professional commitment, his theoretical orientation, and his physical and psychological presence. With the ordinary active therapist, self-disclosure is secondary to his interventions. The indications discussed in this chapter concern self-disclosure as the primary therapeutic agent rather than the byproduct of other types of active intervention. The indications will be discussed in terms of (1) the type and goal of therapy; (2) the real relationship between therapist and patient; (3) the patient's ego strength; (4) the nature of the alliance between patient and therapist; (5) the patient's feelings about the therapist; and (6) the therapist's feelings about the patient.

Type and Goal of Therapy
In this section, the indications for self-disclosure in repressive, ego-supportive, and evocative therapies will be discussed.

REPRESSIVE THERAPIES
Self-disclosure by the leader is a necessity in repressive therapeutic approaches conducted by lay persons in organizations such as Al-

coholics Anonymous and Recovery, Inc. In lay-led therapies, the qualifications for effective leadership are a successful struggle with the problem for which the member also seeks help and a willingness to disclose and discuss this common problem. The leader is a living example that the problem can be overcome, and the task of the group member is to identify with the leader and his way of life. Identification is facilitated through examples of the leader's reactions to, and management of, his own problems. The persons seeking help are then encouraged to try the leader's approach for themselves.

Repressive therapies led by mental health professionals emphasize incorporation of the therapist's instructions and suggestions rather than his person or his way of life. Patients in repressive therapies are not ordinarily concerned with the specifics of the therapist's person. In repressive therapies, the therapist discloses his professional attitudes and opinions and may even give advice, couched in terms of, "What I would do if I were in your shoes . . ." By way of reassurance, the therapist may say, "I've felt the same way myself," or, "Many people I know feel the same way." By reassuring the patient that he is not "different," the therapist draws attention away from unconscious material and facilitates the process of identification, thus reducing the patient's sense of alienation.

Repressive interventions are occasionally necessary in all types of therapy. If a patient is especially anxious during a first visit, it is entirely appropriate for the therapist to comment that he, too, experiences anxiety in an unfamiliar situation. Such a statement helps ease the tension but does not preclude further exploration of the patient's anxiety. At times of overwhelming anxiety in ego-supportive or evocative therapy, the therapist can reassure the patient that in his experience, such emotional storms do not signal an impending loss of contact with reality. Thus, repressive interventions can facilitate nonrepressive forms of therapy.

EGO-SUPPORTIVE THERAPIES
To challenge a pathological ego defense, like a patient's denial of feelings, the therapist may say, "I would have been angry had I been in your shoes." This identification of the therapist with the patient gently pushes aside denial and stimulates less defensiveness than a therapist's comment, "You must have felt something!" By using self-disclosure, the therapist acknowledges the patient's right to be angry rather than implicitly demanding that he be angry, with a statement like, "You must have been angry!"

Feedback in ego-supportive therapies does not require that patient and therapist be equally exposed. In supportive therapies, the therapist makes use of himself as *part* of his professional expertise, not instead of it.

Mrs. U. had been in ego-supportive therapy for several years. She had suffered for many years from concerns about her physical health. She interpreted any ache or pain as a sign of a developing malignancy and was in a state of perpetual doubt as to whether she should see her physician or let herself be eaten up by the imaginary malignancy and end her suffering. I inadvertently compounded her suffering by making occasional sarcastic remarks. She noticed that she felt worse after sessions in which I was irritable and prone to sarcasm. When she told me this, I acknowledged a mean side to my personality and said I felt I could control my meanness with her. She was surprised and pleased. My disclosure, coupled with my promise to deal more effectively with my sarcasm, helped her to work through her idea that psychotherapy was another form of torture that she had to endure. This feedback was helpful because it confirmed her perception of reality and helped her to deal effectively with a situation in real life, thus reducing her sense of helplessness. It did not, on the other hand, require equal exposure, a confession of all the mean deeds I have ever done.

The process of identification with the therapist in ego supportive therapies requires little or no exposure of the therapist's outside life. Patients usually identify with the therapist's inquiring attitude, his optimism, his willingness to face difficulties and misunderstandings that arise in the sessions, his perseverance, and his willingness to assume responsibility for himself. Patients also become aware that the therapist knows his limitations and does not assume responsibility for events that are beyond his control. All of the above-listed attributes of the therapist are readily visible to the patient during the therapeutic hour. So are his shortcomings, which initially trouble patients who wish for an omnipotent therapist. As therapy progresses, the fact of the therapist's minor foibles (wiggling in his chair, pulling his moustache, occasionally chewing on a fingernail) facilitates the process of identification, individuation (I wouldn't want to be completely like him), and ultimate separation.

EVOCATIVE THERAPIES
In evocative therapies, the patient's attention is focused on his inner workings rather than on the reactions or personality of his therapist. If the development and resolution of a transference neurosis is the primary therapeutic vehicle, the therapist needs to be especially careful to maintain his neutrality during the early stages of its evolution. However, the therapist's refusal to express *any* feeling may obstruct therapy. Greenson cites an incident in which a patient of one of his psychoanalytic trainees appeared one day swathed in bandages, as the result of an

automobile accident. His analyst did not respond to this real injury. The patient left the session feeling hurt, humiliated, and angry. The patient's initial impulse was to terminate treatment. He did miss the next several scheduled sessions but returned to treatment reasoning, "Maybe analysts *have* to behave that way." The analysis, however, did not progress to any great depth. Greenson suggests that the analyst's unresponsiveness led the patient to experience his therapist as unfeeling or out of contact, which blocked the development of a trusting atmosphere and a productive treatment relationship.[1]

Greenson and Wexler suggest that one should apologize to a patient for being unnecessarily hurtful and that an apology does not interfere with the therapeutic process. Failure to be forthright in such matters injects an element of hypocrisy and oppressiveness into the therapeutic relationship. Greenson and Wexler also make specific suggestions for the admission of a technical error to a patient. In dealing with a technical error, be it due to countertransference, faulty interpretations, or shortcomings in the therapist's personality, the therapist should give the patient ample opportunity to discover the error himself. The patient's fantasies, before and after the error, are analyzed as well as the patient's reaction to the acknowledgment of the error.[2] Allowing the patient time and opportunity to become aware of the therapist's error encourages the development of his reality testing. Obviously, the impact of the technical error must be ascertained. It may be trivial or overwhelming. If the latter, therapy must temporarily be addressed to helping the patient deal with the psychological trauma. Exploring the patient's reactions to the admission of the error by the therapist uncovers his feelings about the fact that the therapist is not all-wise and that he can admit his fallibility. When treated in this way, missteps by the therapist can be turned into positive growth experiences for patient and therapist alike.

Mrs. A. E., a patient in long-term, intensive psychotherapy, asked what I thought to be the cause of a particular problem. I said that she had never grieved for her father. She was shocked. She said that for years, she had been unable to go to his grave without sobbing uncontrollably. She could not imagine how I had come to that conclusion. I acknowledged that I was mistaken and admitted that I had forgotten. The effect of the error on the patient was trivial in this case. The patient, although shocked by my lapse of memory, was not traumatized. I later reflected on my error and realized that my conclusion was based on her current attitude toward men, not on what she had told me about her feelings concerning her father's death. My presumption that she was still dealing with his death by denial and attempts at substitution was finally confirmed mch later in therapy in relation to another important loss. The denial had occurred in spite of what appeared to be adequate grief and mourning.

In 1912, Freud advised beginning analysts not to deal with resistance by telling patients about their own emotional difficulties or by giving other intimate information about themselves. This, he felt, would substitute a personal relationship that would undermine their working relationship. Freud then states, "the doctor should be impenetrable to the patient and, like a mirror, reflect nothing but what is shown to him."[3] Freud did not mean that the analyst is to be cold or lifeless in demeanor. He was making a broad reference to the long-term goal of treatment, the patient's awareness of his own mind rather than the analyst's mind, and the fact that opening the therapist's mind to the patient can complicate the process.

Stone indicates that in some instances, information about the analyst as a person is helpful. It can correct fragmented or distorted impressions that support tenacious transference resistances. Furthermore, excessive frustration of ordinary curiosity can increase the regressive elements in the transference neurosis to the point that they become difficult to deal with through interpretation. The patient may also feel belittled by the therapist's invulnerability to his aggression and criticism or by the therapist's selective silences. Stone doubts that the course of therapy is seriously affected by knowing whether one vacations in Vermont or Maine or whether one knows more about sailing than golf or bridge. However, it may be harmful if the therapist indicates how well he handled a problem similar to a patient's problem, which the patient himself has handled poorly. The patient thereby feels shamed. The therapist may also burden the patient with a value in life, whether it be physical activity or an appreciation of art, that the patient does not and never will enjoy but nevertheless cherishes because of its value to the therapist.

The psychoanalytic method ordinarily proscribes gratification of the patient's transference wishes. Stone suggests that the patient in an analytically oriented therapy be allowed the "legitimate" transference gratification of experiencing his analyst's physicianly vocation (an integrated, realistic representation of parental functions) to the degree necessary to maintain the therapeutic relationship, without acceding to more primitive, potentially destructive transference wishes. Without some degree of palpable human relationship from the start, the technical difficulties of the treatment become enormous. While it is a hindrance to be anxiously solicitous every time the patient is distressed, it is helpful for the therapist to react as a friendly person at a time of catastrophe for the patient. Absence of a positive response at such times may be destructive. Responding to the patient's anger with anger is obstructive, but it is often useful to express one's irritation when actually victimized by a patient.[4]

If, during the course of treatment, a patient makes a comment about the therapist's style or personality, the therapist has the option of dealing with it as a transference, a resistance, or an objective observation. Failing to deal with some comments as objective observations may be dehumanizing and, ultimately, antitherapeutic. Such evasions can stimulate further questioning by the patient and may ultimately become iatrogenic stumbling blocks, as they did with Viscott, a psychiatrist who reported that his attempt to become a patient in psychoanalysis was aborted by his analyst's refusal to answer personal questions.[5]

It is often valuable for the therapist to introduce a bit of reality about himself to facilitate the resolution of a transference neurosis. A married male therapist, for example, can refrain from correcting a female patient's idea that he is single. This, in turn, allows her to develop a fantasy: that he is unable to form a lasting relationship with a woman, and uses his patients to obtain sublimated sexual gratification. Further exploration reveals her own wish for masochistic submission to a man, based on her wishes toward her father. As she becomes aware of the transference basis of her fantasy, the therapist can reveal that he is married to help speed transference resolution, having accomplished the work of elucidating the patient's feelings toward her father.

Kubie suggests that exposure of the therapist's sense of humor is occasionally helpful. He sees it as most useful in the late stages of a successful therapy, when there is little likelihood that the patient will feel derided.[6] (The use of humor in therapy is discussed in more detail in chapter 7.)

The Real Relationship between Therapist and Patient

The therapist must deal with certain real aspects of his relationship with his patient. The therapist must make it clear when his purpose is evaluation rather than treatment and must make certain that the patient understands when the therapist is acting on behalf of a referring agency. Taking these steps obviates the possibility of betrayal by the therapist or self-betrayal by the patient, since many patients assume that all information is held in confidence. When employed by a mental health agency, the therapist is only indirectly the agent of the patient. When one engages a therapist in private practice, the therapist is in the employ of the patient but is not necessarily the patient's agent. The therapist, in accepting employment, tacitly or explicitly reserves the right *not* to act for the patient, as he sees fit.

It may be reasonable under some circumstances for the therapist to disclose his feelings about performing an evaluation, especially if he is performing under duress or if the evaluation is to satisfy an administrative requirement rather than a need of the patient. If a patient is brought against his will for treatment to an inpatient setting, it is reasonable for the therapist to relate that he, too, would have strong feelings if deprived of freedom in order to help the patient express and work out his feelings.

Whether the patient comes to treatment voluntarily or against his will, the therapist attempts to establish himself as the agent of the health-seeking aspect of the patient. The therapist needs to indicate the degree to which the relationship is confidential and under what circumstances he will breach confidentiality or interfere actively in the patient's life. All this need not be spelled out in the initial interview but will ordinarily have to be dealt with in the course of treatment of more severely disturbed patients.

I told Mrs. X., who was seeking treatment as a means to avoid prosecution for mail fraud, that I would not testify for her in court. I told her that I would consent only to treat her and that if she wished an evaluation in connection with her legal difficulties, she would need to retain the services of another physician.

Mutual trust by patient and therapist is usually tacitly acknowledged.

I told Mrs. X. that in view of her history, I did not feel I could trust her to pay my bill. I required her to pay at each visit and said that I would extend her credit only after I felt I could trust her.

The therapist needs to protect himself emotionally, physically, and financially. Further, it is not in the patient's best interest if he is allowed to gratify himself at the expense of others, including the therapist. The therapist should not disregard the patient's needs, but he need not allow himself to be abused. I self-disclosed to Mr. C., who was threatening my life, to protect myself from his violence and to protect him from the consequences of his own violent act (see p. 60).

All therapists periodically encounter persons whom they cannot treat effectively. A therapist who knows he is ineffective when dealing with problems such as homosexuality or adolescent rebellion owes his patient a referral to a more effective therapist. In such a situation, it is important for the patient to know he is being transferred so that he can receive the best treatment, not because he is undesirable. It is inexcusable to allow a patient to feel he is being transferred because of his undesirability rather than the therapist's limitations. The therapist's personal concern in this situation is to maintain his feeling of potency while recognizing that his knowledge and skills are limited. Therapists' acknowledgment of limitations does no damage to patients or to therapists' reputation. Patients and therapists alike suffer from the therapist's refusal to make such an acknowledgment.

The real relationship between therapist and patient goes through at least three stages; a beginning, a middle, and a termination, which I will present in oversimplified form. The first stage is a getting-acquainted period for patient and therapist alike. The decision about the type of therapy to be employed is made and implemented, and the therapist begins to work through the patient's resistances to cooperation. The first stage may be worked through in less than one session, or it may require many years.

Self-disclosures by the therapist have little place in the early part of the treatment relationship. The therapist cannot know the patient well enough at this point to estimate the probable impact of his disclosures. When early self-disclosures are made, they usually relate more to the personal needs of the therapist than to the treatment needs of the patient. At worst, they suggest vulnerability, self-centeredness, and the wish for self-display; at best, they suggest that the therapist has some difficulty in listening objectively to his patient.

In the middle stage, the work of therapy is accomplished. The patient achieves the degree of insight or control of symptoms possible under the circumstances, introjecting, parroting, or struggling against the values promulgated by the therapist. A part of this process is a series of separation-individuation opportunities in which the patient chooses whether to differentiate as an individual from the therapist. In this middle stage, disclosures by the therapist can help patients appreciate the personal context in which the therapist maintains his value system. As patients come to recognize their potential to become fully individuated persons rather than extensions, pawns, or controllers of those on whom they depend, they pick and choose among the attributes of the therapist with which they wish to identify. There is a danger, however, of identifications with aspects of the therapist that do not constructively augment the patient's personality.

The final stage is letting go of the therapist-patient relationship. Occasionally, it is a letting go of the therapist-patient aspect of the relationship and a move toward a social relationship. The therapist lets the patient know, through self-disclosure, whether the relationship can move toward friendship or will remain therapist-patient, though inactive.

A major crisis in the patient's life, such as the death of a loved one or a severe illness, *may* call for a personal reaction from the therapist.

The timing of the therapist's disclosure of his own feelings depends on the type of treatment employed. In any situation, the patient should be allowed to express his feelings first. Other real occurrences calling for a personal reaction on the part of the therapist are forced interruption of treatment and successful termination of treatment. Again, the patient's feelings come first, but it is reasonable for the therapist to express his own feelings of frustration, anger, or sense of loss afterward.

Ego Strength

The less the patient's ego strength, the greater the likelihood he will be harmed by a therapist's self-disclosure. This danger must be weighed against the fact that patients who are poorly integrated have little tolerance for uncertainty and ambiguity and, therefore, have greater need to know where they stand and what they can expect from their therapists. These patients basically need to know that the therapist is dependable, trustworthy, and personally involved in the treatment process. Concrete questions about age, marital status, number and sex of one's children, and religion need not be sidestepped. These are not intimate disclosures, and they serve primarily to help the patient orient himself to the therapist as a real person. They also do not preclude investigation of the patient's fantasies about the therapist. Being real to patients with little ego strength reduces fantasy and encourages the patient to face the real world. Long suggests that the therapist may expose his personal limitations, attitudes, feelings, and autobiographical material to help a patient undergoing severe ego fragmentation develop an alliance with the therapist as a real person rather than as a projection of his own fears and wishes.[7] Searles shares his fantasies with severely regressed schizophrenics to help them distinguish between reality and fantasy, as mentioned on p. 29.

A disclosure I made to a severely ill woman illustrates some of the principles described above.

I had struggled intermittently for eight years with Mrs. A. A., an ambulatory schizophrenic woman who had undergone numerous brief delusional decompensations during this time. After nearly a year's absence, she was again referred by her husband because of her increasing hostility toward him and an exacerbation of her many phobias, which virtually precluded any activity away from home. Our sessions consisted of dull reiterations of self-help procedures, which she was unable to carry out. After each session, she suffered a delusional preoccupation that some harm would befall her as a result of having talked to me. As I encouraged her to face her fears one day, she asked if I ever experienced fears or intense dislikes. I said, "I don't like celery." Her face lit up and she said, "One day I'll bring a bunch of celery and force you to eat it. Then you'll understand what I feel!"

My revelation stimulated a momentarily more positive interchange in which she felt more a partner and less a psychopathological specimen. Unfortunately, the mutually participant exchange for which I had hoped did not come about. My disclosure came at a point where she had been unusually interpersonally bold, engaging in quite uncharacteristic flirting and teasing, and skirting dangerously close to her underlying sexual feelings. Soon, she retreated into greater belligerence toward her husband and required protracted hospitalization.

Hill, in describing the psychotherapeutic approach to schizophrenia, suggests that the human interest, concern, curiosity, warmth, and helpfulness are most safely and satisfactorily expressed by the therapist in what he calls an "intransitive" mood. The patient needs to feel these qualities in his therapist without any sense that they are being imposed upon him or that demands (like reciprocity) that he cannot meet are being made. The therapist allows himself to be aware of his erotic interests, anger, amusement, fatigue, and so forth, but these are also best kept intransitive, that is, not aimed at the patient.[8]

The therapist can afford relative openness with well-integrated patients once they are past their omnipotent expectations of him. Since there is little likelihood of damaging the patient, the therapist can relax and be himself if he chooses. Many therapist elect this comfortable style of relating, which they find less draining than being neutral or only selectively self-disclosing. They develop real, mutually supportive relationships with their patients and feel enhanced rather than worn out at the end of the working day. This is particularly true of marathon group therapists, for whom psychotherapy sessions are often an important part of their own emotional lives. Many therapists become social friends of their patients at the end of therapy. Such friendships are mutually gratifying, but they make the resumption of further psychotherapy difficult. Before allowing a friendship to develop, the therapist must ask himself if he is willing to relinquish his patient as a patient *forever*.

The Patient-Therapist Alliance

The primary area of alliance between patient and therapist varies from time to time during treatment. The therapist may ally with the mature, self-observing part of his patient, the self-critical part, the patient's instinctual urges, or the patient's pathological defenses against self-criticism or unconscious drives. The patient may ally with any of the above aspects of his therapist. The ideal alliance is between the mature, self-observing aspects of both the patient and the therapist. When this occurs, the therapist's disclosures are information to be used or rejected according to the patient's mature assessment of its value, as in the example of Mrs. F. (see chapter 2, p. 27). One can also establish a mature alliance with many regressed patients. Moreover, disclosure of one's self as a person may provide an important avenue for establishing a mature link with the severely emotionally ill.

McDanald reported on a severely depressed 250-pound woman who had made serious suicidal threats. After three months of treatment, which seemed more social than therapeutic, she joyously plumped herself into his lap saying, "I've been thinking of doing this all week." After noticing his expression, she commented, "You don't look very comfortable." Without hesitation, McDanald opined, "I don't believe I'm mature enough to work with you in my lap." She exclaimed, "Oh, I'm so glad to hear you say that you don't feel you are completely mature." Shortly after his disclaimer of complete maturity, the patient became less withdrawn, depressed, and suicidal. McDanald presumed he had reduced her sense of alienation through identification with him, fostered by his statement which allowed her to feel that they had at least one attribute in common.[9]

The Patient's Feelings about the Therapist

Self-disclosure is most useful as a facilitating process when therapist and patient are aware of and have partly worked through some of the patient's transference expectations. In repressive therapies, it is sufficient for the therapist to be aware of the transference situation and to gratify and frustrate as the situation indicates. In supportive therapies, such disclosures can heighten identification with the therapist. In evocative therapies, the disclosures can provide a vehicle to examine tranference distortions.

Let us take, as an example, the patient's wish for an omnipotent parent. In a repressive therapy, the therapist may refer to a lecture he has given or his academic title as a means of partially gratifying the patient's wish and encouraging his dependency on the therapist's judgment. Allowing a patient in ego-supportive therapy access to a little-known positive aspect of the therapist, such as a scientific paper that he has written, suggests taking the patient into the therapist's inner world as one who can appreciate and share the therapist's scientific accomplishment. This allows him closeness to the omnipotent parent, but more as a peer than as a protected child. Disclosure of the therapist's noteworthy accomplishments to a patient in an evocative therapy is followed by an examination of the patient's reactions and associations to allow eventual interpretation of the patient's wish for an omnipotent parent.

Self-disclosures can be used to bring out positive or negative feelings about the therapist. Such manipulations are valid only if they highlight an existing feeling state. They should not be used to induce feelings; this changes the therapeutic situation from one of cooperation to one in which the patient is the puppet of the therapist.

Disclosures can help patients who use neutrality toward the therapist as a defense against feelings, be they positive, negative, aggressive, sexual, or dependent. Given a patient of adequate ego strength and a good working alliance, the therapist can reveal some of his thoughts or feelings to help the patient become aware of hitherto unconscious feelings. However, the therapist must be aware that a patient's seeming neutrality can be a major defense against feelings that would make treatment even more difficult and must respect the defense until the patient is strong enough to relinquish it.

The Therapist's Feelings about the Patient

The most therapeutic feeling the therapist can convey to his patient is, "I respect you as a person." The therapist's respect does not license the patient to behave entirely as he wishes during the therapeutic session; it is not unconditional acceptance. Unconditional acceptance would not only be unreasonable but unfeasible. The therapist must react directly against certain behaviors of the patient, especially those which endanger himself or others. The therapist's regard for himself is demonstrated by his unwillingness to be unnecessarily endangered by his patient. The patient should eventually identify with and incorporate this sense of self-respect. Respect is a form of acceptance that recognizes the uniqueness of an individual and gives cognizance to his needs and wishes. It is possible to respect a person without liking him, but it is difficult to behave respectfully toward a person whom one actively dislikes.

Respect can be conveyed in many ways. Respect for patients is best conveyed nonverbally, by the therapist's attitude toward the patient—his way of greeting the patient, of entering the room with the patient, of interacting with the patient, and his way of terminating the sessions. When the therapist uses an adult patient's first name, he may be suggesting a warm, personal relationship, but this type of intimacy may also suggest little regard for the patient as an adult. When the therapist jokes with a patient, he may be conveying his own comfort in the relationship. However, he may also be indicating little regard for the patient's feelings. A respectful attitude makes no presumptions. It does not take a patient's feelings or reactions for granted. It acknowledges the patient's right to feel differently at different times. It is based on a willingness to be sensitive to the patient that is not obscured by the therapist's need to experience his patient in a certain way.

Mintz uses touching to display respect and concern for patients undergoing particularly trying times in therapy or in their life situations, but she is aware that touching can be readily misconstrued.[10] Robertiello uses total self-disclosure to convey his respect for the ability of his patients in groups to help each other and him.[11]

Ordinarily, communication of respect for the patient involves little disclosure of the therapist. The same is true of the therapist's concern for the welfare of his patients. There is little need, under ordinary circumstances, for the therapist to dramatize his concern beyond his general attentiveness and willingness to interact with and respond to the patient. Verbalizations of concern are of less use than appropriate actions by the therapist.

Expressions of liking or of anger have little place early in therapy. Patients in the initial stages of therapy are prone to experience anger as a confirmation of their worthlessness. They interpret shows of positive feelings as indicators of acceptable behavior. It then becomes difficult to help the patient seek what is best for himself rather than try to please the therapist.

An early disclosure of my feelings was useful with Mrs. A. B., a woman with moderately severe characterological and neurotic problems, who had been treated previously by two other therapists. She had some success with her first therapist; she had been able to face some traumatic material from childhood. Her experience with her second therapist reenacted her intensely positive and negative feelings toward her father; she was unable to make any headway because of her perception of the therapist as harsh, critical, and controlling.

In our relationship, I responded in a positive way to her vivaciousness. She was aware of my response and asked, during our second session, if I liked her. I said, "Yes." She said she didn't understand how someone could like a person as worthless as herself. I shrugged and said, "I just do!" My open positive response served as a foundation for separating her transference reactions from her perceptions of me as a real person, which facilitated a constructive process of self-observation instead of self-criticism.

There is need for caution when the patient actively solicits expressions of the therapist's feelings toward him. Caution is also merited when the therapist feels strongly impelled to reveal his own feelings. Expressions of feelings of liking, regret toward, anger with, and sexual attraction to patients are double-edged. It is probably more useful to speak of liking a certain aspect of a patient than to speak of liking the patient as a whole; realistically, no one is totally likable at all times. Under certain circumstances, such as Searles' sharing of fantasy to help a schizophrenic woman distinguish fact from fantasy, it is useful to express sexual attraction toward a patient. I have found this useful in the middle stages of treatment of some neurotic patients.

With two women, the need for sexual acceptance by men was an important aspect of their emotional difficulties. In each case, acknowledging my sexual attraction helped them work through their wishes to experience me as a real sexual object. In both cases, physical contact had been the chief means by which they obtained acceptance while avoiding the regressive, infantile aspects of their wish for closeness. I made it clear with both that I would not physically express my feelings toward them. They tested me, came to accept my wishes, were complimented by my attraction to them, and felt that continuation of therapy was more important than pressing for physical intimacy with me.

The expression of negative (hostile, angry) feelings toward patients can be useful only when the patient's self-esteem is adequate and when the patient can understand that his therapist's anger does not mean he is wrong or of little worth. It may be better to express anger with a part of the patient or a specific act of the patient rather than to say, "I am angry with you." The principal use for expressing anger is in dealing with conscious manipulation by the patient who is accustomed to taking advantage of others. The therapist's anger helps sensitize the patient to his own behavior.

Summary

There is general agreement that the effective psychotherapist feels and somehow transmits respect and concern for his patients. Direct verbal assurances are seldom necessary. Ordinarily, patients sense enough of the therapist's concern to enable them to tolerate the frustrating aspects of the therapeutic relationship. The degree, manner, and circumstances under which therapists display concern, or other aspects of themselves, are highly controversial and largely represent the range of needs of psychotherapists.

Personal disclosures by the therapist can serve the treatment needs of patients in many ways. In repressive therapies, they can shore up the patient's sense of himself as a human being. In supportive therapies, disclosures can provide interpersonal feedback and a reasonable model for identification. In evocative therapies, the resolution of transference can be enhanced.

Open discussion of the real relationship between therapist and patient helps to maintain realistic expectations of one another, prevents betrayal of the patient, and helps the patient to maintain his dignity when transfer to another therapist is required.

Disclosures may be especially useful in the treatment of severely ill patients to help distinguish fact from fantasy, to indicate acceptance of the patient as a person, and to establish the existence of the therapist as a separate individual when the patient's ego boundaries are weak.

The most therapeutically useful disclosures are made during contact between the mature, observing aspect of the therapist and the mature self-observing aspect of the patient. Disclosures are best withheld when the patient needs to avoid a personal relationship with the therapist, and when the patient's positive or negative feelings about the therapist are intense. Attempts to manipulate such feeling states by self-disclosures are dangerous.

The therapist owes his patients respect but cannot deliver unconditional acceptance. Expressions of positive, negative, and even sexual feelings all have a place in psychotherapeutic relationships, as does expression of the therapist's intuitive awareness. All, however, must be in an appropriate context.

In outline, self-disclosure can be useful to

1. enhance the patient's reality testing by defining the therapist as a real person and by defining the real patient-therapist relationship
2. heighten the patient's self-esteem by conveying respect and facilitate identification with a respected person (the therapist)
3. provide feedback about the impact of the patient on others
4. promote identification with positive aspects of the therapist, for example, his calmness, reasonableness, and interpersonal skills
5. sufficiently gratify a patient's transference and object needs to establish and maintain a therapeutic alliance
6. resolve certain transference resistances.

The absolute indications for self-disclosure by the therapist are

1. to preserve the life of the patient or the therapist

2. to deal with significant alterations in the therapeutic relationship produced by events in the therapist's outside life

3. to work out disruptions in therapy produced by some aspect of the therapist as a person.

References

1. Greenson, R. R.: Beyond transference and interpretation. *Internat. J. Psychoanalysis* 53:213–217, 1972.

2. Greenson, R. R., and Wexler, M.: The non-transference relationship in the psychoanalytic situation, *Internat. J. Psychoanalysis* 50:27–39,.1969.

3. Freud, S.: Recommendations for physicians on the psychoanalytic method of treatment. *Sigmund Freud: Collected Papers,* trans. by J. Riviere. Basic Books, New York, 1959, pp. 323–333.

4. Stone, L.: *The Psychoanalytic Situation.* International Universities Press, New York, 1961.

5. Viscott, D.: *The Making of a Psychiatrist.* Arbor House, 1972.

6. Kubie, L. S.: The destructive potential of humor in psychotherapy, *Am. J. Psychiatry* 127:861–866, 1971.

7. Long, R. T.: Personal communication, 1970.

8. Hill, L. B.: *Psychotherapeutic Intervention in Schizophrenia.* Chicago, University of Chicago Press, 1955.

9. McDanald, E. C.: The schizoid problem—special therapeutic techniques. Address to the North Texas Psychiatric Society, March, 1970.

10. Mintz, E. E.: *Marathon Groups: Reality and Symbol.* Appleton-Century-Crofts, New York, 1971.

11. Robertiello, R. C.: The leader in a "leaderless" group. *Psychother. Theor. Res. Prac.* 9:259–261, 1972.

7

The Pitfalls of Therapeutic Openness

There are many possible misuses of self-disclosure. Understandably, mental health professionals are reluctant to publish accounts of their errors, so the literature on the subject is sparse. A damaging self-disclosure can obstruct or reverse progress toward the therapeutic goal in many ways. It can undermine the relationship between patient and therapist, render the patient less able to cope with the real world or his feelings, or stimulate those aspects of himself with which he is least able to deal. It can block the therapist's awareness of his own feelings or result in expressions of feelings that undermine the patient's self-esteem.

The therapist may self-disclose inappropriately to be honest, to manipulate a patient for his own gratification, or to obtain psychological help from his patients. Disclosing can also help the therapist avoid dealing with material from the patient that provokes his own anxiety. From the patient's point of view, the therapist may supply gratifications that heighten resistance to change, clinging, demands for further gratification, and action as a means of warding off disquieting thoughts and feelings.

The Problem of Honesty

Lieberman's study of encounter groups demonstrates that total honesty with patients is not a virtue.[1] Carkhuff found that low levels of genuineness impede therapy, but also found that very high levels of genuineness did not augment client functioning. He suggests that genuineness is not a license for free expression of feelings by the therapist, especially feelings of hostility toward the patient.[2] The therapist is obliged to control his reactions to patients and does so at the point where he is aware that his response is highly idiosyncratic and likely to damage the patient's self-esteem.

Therapists do owe their patients certain honest disclosures. The patient is entitled to know his therapist's professional credentials, his areas of expertise, and whether the therapist has adequate professional interest in him to undertake his treatment. Physicians or state-certified psychologists are legally required to display a license to practice. Such licensure indicates recognized expertise but cannot guarantee success because many of the factors that determine success or failure of treatment are unpredictable, unmeasurable, and unknowable. Honest statements about professional expertise and interests can be made to a mildly troubled person seeking outpatient treatment. This type of honesty is not appropriate with a patient suffering a severe, agitated depression who must be hospitalized to avert a suicide attempt. The person whose life is in danger must be reassured of the effectiveness of treatment. Any hint of doubt will increase the likelihood of a suicide attempt or of resistance to hospitalization.

Patients often ask, "Doctor, what chance of successful treatment do *I* have with you?" Frequently, the patient asks this question before the therapist has sufficient information to make an intelligent estimate. The therapist must defer his answer until he has enough information about the patient and has probed the question adequately to determine an appropriate response. The question is not only a request for information; it also tests the therapist's sense of adequacy. Most patients are satisfied by a statement that the therapist regards himself as generally competent.

If the therapist acknowledges good results treating patients with similar problems, he must be aware of the pitfalls. For example, the patient may come to rely on the therapist for a magical cure rather than face the need for involvement in therapy. Or he may blame himself instead of the therapist if the treatment goes poorly. If, on the other hand, the therapist says he has not had good results, he may appear incompetent or intensify the patient's fears.

To have a workable treatment relationship, the patient must feel that the therapist is real, is emotionally attuned to him, and is interested in him as a person, but this need not be conveyed explicitly.

The therapist's honesty is a tool whose use is based on the therapeutic need of the patient. Therapist and patient are in an unequal relationship in which the patient temporarily relinquishes certain rights in exchange for therapeutic gain. It is in the patient's best interest for the therapist to be self-aware, but it is not in his patient's best interest to convey his full self at all times. Therapists are emotional beings like their patient, but there is more to therapy than revealing the eccentricities of one to the other. Being as irrational (or "human") as one's patients negates therapeutic effectiveness.[3] It is like telling the patient that he is no worse off than anybody else (including the therapist) and, therefore, should be happy with his lot. When the therapist allows himself free expression to his patients, he becomes totally dependent on mutual consensus, which facilitates acting out, instead of exploring unconsciously determined behavior.

The Therapist's Sense of Humor

The use of humor in therapy can be antitherapeutic. Kubie feels that humor circumvents two important protections for the patient, the therapist's incognito and the separation between a social and a professional relationship. Since the therapist is in a position of authority in relation to his patient, he can project his difficulties onto his patient in a "humorous" way that increases the patient's vulnerability and uses him as a scapegoat. Sharing of humor blunts the therapist's self-observation and also enhances, as does a sharing of grief, a powerful emotional tie between patient and therapist. Hence, humor is especially tempting for the relatively constricted, sober, humorless therapist, who thus allows himself a form of self-display. It lowers the barriers against acting out the therapist's unconscious feelings toward the patient and is perhaps the most seductive form of "transference wooing." Every patient is in pain. To be viewed with charm and easy humor often compounds it.[4]

My own experience largely corroborates Kubie's view. A substantial number of the humorous remarks I make to patients to lessen the tension during the hour fall flat or intensify the emotional tenseness of the situation. Many of my humorous interventions are countertransference-based or related to my mood. On the other hand, I have seen no damage arise from openly enjoying an event that the patient presents as humorous.

Occasionally, I will ask one of my more constricted, humorless patients if he sees any humor in a series of events he has just described. If he cannot, I do not persist. If he can, I use his ability to see the humor in what he has described as a possible alternative to his usual overly serious, destructively self-analytic reactions to life circumstances.

Manipulation of Patients' Feelings

I have found no reports on the negative aspects of manipulating patients' feelings. I have experimented with expressing my feelings to provoke patients to anger or sadness when I felt they would profit from a catharsis of feelings. I have found that such provocations do not relieve symptoms. In fact, they compound the patient's problems. Formerly suffering as a result of his own internal turmoil, the patient now also suffers as the result of external pressure from his therapist. His previously unrecognized grief or anger now appears to stem from the therapist's behavior toward him. The patient can react in three ways. He can project his emotional difficulties onto the therapist and feel persecuted in the treatment relationship, he can defend himself by discontinuing treatment, or he can tell the therapist that he does not appreciate his provocation.

The last alternative is the only positive outcome I have seen from attempting to manipulate patients' feelings. In the course of treatment, certain patients who have had the experience of being manipulated "for their own good" rejected this position and began to work toward a cooperative relationship in which they shared the responsibility for ascertaining and setting forth their own feelings.

A therapist may self-disclose to demonstrate hitherto unrecognized feelings in his patient. For example, a patient who experiences himself as unemotional may be brought to tears by a therapist's self-revelation. Attempting, in this or other ways, to actively breach a patient's defenses often points to an exaggerated need of the therapist to prove his potency through immediate, dramatic measures. This active breaching of defenses can have unfortunate consequences. It removes the patient's responsibility for lowering his own defenses, that is, cooperating in the treatment relationship. It stimulates dependence on the therapist's resources and encourages the patient to view the therapist as omnipotent. Attempts by the therapist to further manipulate the patient become less and less effective as the patient learns more effective countermanipulations. The magic-craving patient is forced to make escalating demands on the therapist to assert his superhuman potency, which eventuates in a suicide attempt or a regression to a state of psychological immobilization. In extreme instances the result can be total neutralization of the therapist's effectiveness through a profound regression that can only be reversed by separating the patient from the therapist whose omnipotent needs contributed to the patient being overwhelmed by infantile cravings for nurturance.[5]

Gratification of the Therapist

Therapists can self-disclose to obtain physical and psychological gratification from their patients. Situations of this sort are usually not unilateral. They are most often the result of a collusion to avoid or postpone working out a problem and to substitute some form of mutual gratification. The therapist consciously or unconsciously sides with the patient's resistance, whether the resistance is an ego defense mechanism such as rationalization, a superego mandate satisfied by a sadomasochistic relationship between therapist and patient, or an id resistance of mutual libidinal gratification.

The therapist can satisfy his need to feel knowledgeable by spending inordinate amounts of time helping the patient rationalize his situation and feelings with little or no positive change—what Eric Berne has called the game of "Psychiatry."[6]

It is also possible to sustain a sublimated sadomasochistic relationship in which the therapist has the gratification of making interpretations in the form of painful accusations which "wound" the patient, who keeps coming back for more.[7]

Freud and others predicted that minor libidinal gratifications between therapist and patient will lead to the ultimate in physical gratification—sexual intercourse. Reports of sexual relations between therapist and patient are frequent on the newsstands and are now beginning to be discussed in the scientific literature.

Erotic behavior with patients is by no means rare. Of 114 male psychiatrists who responded to a questionnaire concerning erotic practices with patients, 6 stated that they engaged in erotic behavior, including intercourse, with patients.[8] All of these physicians reported their erotic involvement with patients to be rare or occasional. In no case did the physician indicate that he was gratifying his own needs.

Reasons given were, "improves sexual maladjustment," "helps patients' recognition of their sexual status," "especially in the depressed, middle-aged female who feels undesirable," "to relieve frustration in a widow or divorcée who hasn't yet reengaged in dating," and "in healthy patients by mutual consent making the therapy go faster, deeper, and increases dreams." In contrast to the questionnaire study in which the respondents indicated that erotic practices were carried out in the patients' interest, every detailed case report available suggests that the therapist's needs have played a prominent part.

Chesler interviewed eleven women who had had sexual relations with their therapist during or outside of the therapeutic situation.[9] One of these women had attempted to sue a former therapist with whom she allegedly had sexual relations under the guise of treatment. Interestingly enough, the husbands of the four married women in the group were concomitantly seeing the same therapist. Two doctors had created patriarchal "families" with many "wives" (female patients, legal wives, mistresses). Each was married, had a poor relationship with his wife, and was perceived by his patients as a poor lover. Both apparently had sex with as many of their female patients, simultaneously, as they could. The women tended to blame themselves for any "mistreatment" by men; those over the age of thirty-five insisted *they* were to blame.

Even though many of the women felt mistreated, it was generally the therapist who ended the affair. Two of the women reacted with severe depression, one attempted suicide. A fourth woman's husband, in treatment with his wife's therapist, killed himself shortly after he found out about the affair. Chesler's psychodynamic objection to affairs between female patients and male therapists is that they reinforce the notion that "feminine" means to love Daddy, and they violate the incest taboo.

Shepard reviewed eleven cases of homosexual and heterosexual activity between patient and therapist. Not all of the patients felt that they had been harmed. The reports of the various liaisons indicated that the therapists were actively seeking to sexually exploit their patients. It is difficult to see how the therapist aided any of the patients beyond what they could have experienced with an unpaid lover. Shepard concluded that sexual intimacy has the potential for harm as well as help and particularly cautioned prospective patients against therapists who appear too possessive or personally needy of their patients.[10]

Dahlberg studied nine cases in which sexual intimacy was suggested by the therapist or actually occurred between therapist and patient. In eight cases, the therapist was a man in his forties or fifties involved with a younger woman. The ninth case was a homosexual approach by a male therapist. Generally, action was initiated by the therapist to meet his own needs. Several therapists were in great emotional and interpersonal need. Some were in precarious psychological balance. One subsequently suffered an agitated depression. The majority of patients suffered emotionally afterward, primarily from a sense of betrayal. Dahlberg suggests that sexual exploitation by the therapist is more damaging than other types of exploitation, such as through the therapist's laziness or financial greed. While he does not deny that therapists experience many kinds of feelings toward their patients, he questions filling the gap between therapist and patient in a way that can only diminish the objectivity of the therapist and violate the trust of the patient.[11]

Treatment for the Therapist

The therapist is entitled to receive help with his personal problems just as much as his patient. However, if the therapist charges for his services, he is contracting to place the needs of his patient first, and obligating himself to deal with his own problems so that they do not detract from the best possible treatment for the patient. The studies by Dahlberg, Chesler, and Shepard show that the therapist was frequently needier than his patients. Most of the therapists in Dahlberg's study were experiencing life crises of varying severity. Chesler's therapists were frequently sexually inept and inadequate.

Perls gives a poignant example of his attempt to deal with his own severe psychological decompensation through an open, intimate relationship with a patient.[12]

Perls, a physician, interrupted his psychoanalytic training in 1933 to escape the Nazi regime. He was practicing psychotherapy in Miami, Florida, in 1956. After having become increasingly uncomfortable with his wife, he involved himself at age 59 in

> love affairs without any deep emotional involvements. An involvement finally happened in Miami with Marty.
>
> I found you [Marty] despondent, nearly suicidal, disappointed in your marriage. . . . I was proud to take you up and to mold you to my and your needs. You loved and admired me as a therapist and at the same time, became my therapist, cutting with your cruel honesty through my phoniness, bullshit and manipulations. Never was so much equal give and take between us as then. Then came the time when I took you to Europe. Paris, some insane jealousy bouts on my part. . . . Back in Miami I became more and more possessive. My jealousy reached truly psychotic proportions.

At that time, Perls spent many hours each day checking up on Marty and was unable to concentrate in her absence. She took up with another man. Perls attempted suicide. He recovered from his self-inflicted knife wound, became more emotionally stable, and was finally able to work through the separation.

Most patients are not in a position to recommend therapy for a therapist who is in psychological difficulty. They are more likely to be drawn into the therapist's pathology or to react against it by terminating treatment.

The therapist can use his patient to help deal with certain of his own feelings. Therapeutic "honesty" can allow the therapist to discharge hostile feelings in the therapy hour rather than toward the real object of his feelings. It can also help the therapist deal with his own self-punishing tendencies. The disclosure and working out of errors made by the therapist can be useful for the patient, but the therapist can disclose his errors to assuage his guilt, or to receive punishment. In any of these cases, the therapist increases the patient's burden by making himself the patient's responsibility.

When the therapist uses the patient to support his self-esteem, for expiation of guilt, or for punishment, difficulties arise. To avoid these pitfalls, Greenson has made specific suggestions for the admission of a technical error to a patient (see chapter 5).[13]

The therapist can defend himself against stimulation of his own anxiety by presenting occurrences or feelings from his own life similar to those of the patient. This reassures both the patient and himself that nothing out of the ordinary is going on and, therefore, needs no further investigation.

If the therapist lacks the training to help face and work through the conflicts that underlie the patient's difficulties, the therapist can defend against his own technical inadequacy by using self-disclosure to help alleviate the patient's anxiety.

Reinforcement of Resistance

In certain situations, the therapist's use of himself has momentary positive value but also has longer-term negative results.

To demonstrate his human concern, Greenson made a postpartum hospital visit and a subsequent home visit to an analytic patient whose husband had died during her pregnancy. He then had to face the heighted resistance caused by the woman's exaggerated perception of him as saintly, self-sacrificing, and extraordinarily compassionate. This distortion had to be worked through before she could begin to deal with her underlying rage toward her mother, whom she had experienced as unreliable.

Greenson also suggests that the therapist's positive reactions to the patient's insights or therapeutic gain can reduce the potential of therapy as a growth experience by making the therapist's approval the patient's reward. This reinforces the parent-child nature of the relationship and leads to a game of pleasing the therapist.[14] This results in the patient parroting the therapist's view of his psychodynamics or blindly following the therapist's suggestions without developing the ability to adapt this information to fit changing life situations. Patients with the greatest fear of criticism are the ones who most frequently develop this sort of resistance. The more they resemble the therapist and his view of the world, the less the likelihood of criticism. After all, how can the therapist criticize someone so like himself?

Symbiotic Transference

Silverman agrees that therapists must experience empathy but feels that expressions of empathy must be limited. He suggests that the expression of empathy may lead to a "symbiotic transference reaction," a rearousal of feelings and experiences from that period of infancy when differentiation from one's mother was incomplete. The infant, during this period, is deeply dependent on its mother and is presumed to experience a sense of oneness with her, which, if responded to appropriately, creates a feeling of being protected and cared for. This type of relationship can make aggressive feelings toward the therapist inaccessible to the patient. It is as if the patient says, "Since you and I are one, I cannot be angry with you or I will hurt me." An empathic response can obstruct therapy by reducing the patient's anxiety. Without anxiety there is little motivation for change and less possibility for the patient to have a full experiential understanding of his psychopathology. When a therapist's basic stance is overt empathy, the patient may experience confrontation as esteem-lowering criticism rather than neutral or objective observation of the patient and his behavior.

Another problem related to the symbiotic transference occurs when symbiotic wishes are aroused in a person struggling to free himself from a "symbiotic fixation." Silverman defines a symbiotic fixation as a clinging to prevent abandonment; he contrasts it with a symbiotic defense, such as an attempt to ward off hostile feelings through a sense of fusion with the therapist. The symbiotically fixated patient requires the transference gratification of the therapist's empathy, but the therapist must be able to exercise restraint and be neutral when the patient is ready to move beyond the symbiotic stage.[15]

Problems of Physical Contact

In a review of the use of physical contact in psychoanalysis, Mintz notes Freud's urging that "the patient be kept in a state of abstinence or unrequited love . . . The more affection you allow him the more readily you reach his complexes, but the less definite the result." Mintz feels physical contact is inadvisable if it only gratifies, or if it fosters, interminable treatment. According to Mintz, the therapist's touch must not suggest sexual foreplay or give realistic grounds to expect fuller gratification.[16]

Unquestionably, many of the patients who become sexually involved with their therapists are spurred on by therapist-initiated physical contact. The patient who is encouraged to act by virtue of a suggestive touch or statement also runs the risk of being humiliated when he responds, only to find the therapist coolly analyzing the *patient's* sexual interest in him. If the therapist denies his provocation, the patient may be enraged or feel ashamed, his reality testing undermined and his self-esteem injured.

Searles makes the following observations on physical contact:

> *A therapist who is neurotically afraid of physical contact with people . . . to that degree complicates the recovery process in the patient; but so does the therapist who recurrently needs to reassure himself on his own living humanness, his own capacity for feeling, by a dramatically "curative" employment of physical contact with the patient. In the latter instance, it is only ostensibly the trembling and frightened patient who is being helped by the therapist's reassuring touch; covertly the patient is thereby reassuring the therapist of the latter's own capacity for life and lovingness.*[17]

Physical contact may intensify the patient's feelings to the point that therapy can be significantly impaired.

McDanald interrupted a hospitalized patient's catatonic trance by putting his arm around her. She subsequently incorporated him into her fantasy life, developed the delusion that they were overwhelmingly in love with each other, and "took license to express her consuming devotion at the end of each hour through physical clinging, pecking, and later in attempts at passionate kissing which [McDanald] forbade." The patient intermittently developed insight into the fact that she had been "milking" him for everything she could get. However, she eventually required rehospitalization and electroshock. She continued in psychotherapy with McDanald until she splintered an ashtray and cut herself while in his office. She was rehospitalized under another therapist's care, at McDanald's request, but insisted on working with him again after discharge from the hospital. At the time McDanald reported this case, the patient still embraced him at the end of the hour but was no longer clinging or making special demands. When she restarted therapy with him after her third hospitalization, she commented, "Don't ever give a baby a stick of candy unless you are prepared to give the whole box."[18]

Gratification of the Patient

Supplying certain real needs of the patient, such as approval or affection, makes it difficult for the patient to relinquish the therapist, especially if the patient has insufficient supplies of approval or affection outside the therapeutic situation. The patient may have little stimulus to develop other sources of real satisfaction precisely because the therapist has been willing to supply them. Therapists can develop warm, mutually satisfying friendships with patients. Some therapists and patients fall in love and marry. The possibility of real friendship and adult love between therapist and patient cannot be discounted, but it must not be mistaken for the situation in which the patient feels that the therapist is the only friend he can have, the only person he can love, or the only one from whom he can receive love.

Active, affective involvement with patients has great limitations. Emotional involvement can not only contribute to a stalemate in treatment, as it did with Mrs. L. (see chapter 3), but it can help provoke profound psychological decompensation by simultaneously stimulating the patient's wish for and his fear of engulfment or annihilation. Patients with the least tolerance for closeness often press the therapist the most strongly.[19]

In my own experience, the development of intense romantic and sexual feelings in patients who are having difficulty coping with day-to-day living is a thin disguise for strong feelings of hatred projected onto the therapist. Rather than reacting with counterhatred, as many borderline patients do, these patients react with exaggerated love and clinging as an attempt to evade the sadism that they project onto the therapist. These individuals often give a history of severe physical and psychological abuse by their parents, which leads the therapist to perceive their reactions as based on transference rather than projective identification, a mechanism that will be dealt with extensively in chapter 9, which deals with the borderline patient. The importance of this distinction is that transference interpretations do not resolve the clinging based on projective identification; repeatedly pointing out the patient's underlying anger does. In these difficult situations, the therapist does not become aloof, emotionally withdrawn, or detached. Instead, he acknowledges that he cares but maintains that it is his right and the patient's need that the relationship be conducted in a neutral, professional manner.

Some patients whose reality testing seems intact, whose object relations seem sound, and who are not currently deprived of interpersonal needs will press for open displays of the therapist's favor. These requests are sometimes transference-based. More commonly, they are made by individuals with little hope or motivation for change or little faith in therapy. They are quite willing to settle for short-term gratification because they expect no long-term gain to result from allowing themselves to be sufficiently frustrated to examine themselves. Rather than comply with the seemingly innocent request of a fairly healthy person for an honest declaration of the therapist's feelings, it makes more sense to focus on his motivation for asking. This will usually lead to the termination of an unmotivated patient, which is much more desirable than a prolonged impasse. It will also uncover the negative feelings and the sense of hopelessness of the individuals who feel that they or their situation cannot be changed, paving the way for a frank discussion of their misgivings and their prospects for change.

A unique study involving gratification of patients' sexual needs was reported in 1966 by McCartney, who presented data from 1500 "psychoanalyses" conducted over forty years.[20] He claimed that of the approximately 800 female patients who underwent his psychoanalytic therapy, 75 percent made good adjustments. His treatment ranged from 30 to 309 sessions, with an average of 89 sessions, extending from 8 to 59 months. Thirty percent of the adult women sat in his lap, held his hand, or hugged and kissed him. "About 10 percent found it necessary to act out extremely, such as mutual undressing, genital manipulation, or coitus." For his therapeutic rationale, McCartney cited Reich:

> This overt transference which goes with the genital concentration of the libido is the most potent factor in bringing to the surface unconscious material. The genital excitation which arises on the basis of this transference reactivates the original sexual conflict, but many patients refuse

for a long time to recognize the transference character of this situation. The important thing is that in this process they learn to tolerate genital frustration, that for the first time they do not react with disappointment, and they do not regress. They concentrate both emotional and somatic strivings on the analyst. Patients who fail to go through such Overt Transference of a genital character do not succeed in fully establishing genital primacy. In such cases, the analyst has either not succeeded in really liberating from repression the sexual strivings, or he has not succeeded in dissolving the guilt feelings.[21]

McCartney saw sexual intimacy as the way to work through the erotic transference with some patients and blocks in sexual maturation with others. He reported no negative reactions. He said that his method required great maturity on the part of the analyst and indicated that the therapist must refrain at some point from continued sexual intimacy lest the patient's further emotional growth be thwarted. He also suggested that the less mature therapist adhere to the classical "mirror" technique advocated by Freud.

In his paper, McCartney somehow separates physical intimacy from emotional intimacy. It is difficult to see how therapist or patient could be sufficiently objective under these circumstances to determine the right point at which to begin or end sexual intimacy. It is possible, of course, that, after having once experienced physical intimacy with McCartney, it was easy for most of his patients to relinquish him.

Summary

Being real with patients is risky, unless the patient is sensible, sophisticated, and well able to defend himself. Under these circumstances, the patient can reject the less helpful aspects of the therapist and accept the beneficial aspects. It's hard to hurt healthy people. On the other hand, it is easy to shortchange, extract from, and damage the ordinary person who seeks help with emotional problems. He enters therapy because he is not well able to defend himself or because his defenses themselves have disabled him. Having the additional burden of relating to the therapist as a person seems an unreasonable demand of the patient who first enters therapy. Use of self by the therapist can lead to an impasse or worsening of the patient's condition under the following circumstances:

1. when it is an attempt to manipulate or seduce an unmotivated or unprepared patient into therapy
2. when it is a manipulation of a patient's feelings
3. when it is designed to meet the therapist's needs, be they social, sexual, or psychological
4. when it is an outlet for the therapist's feelings without reference or relevance to the need of the patient
5. when it is the therapist's attempt to defend against his own feelings
6. when it helps the therapist avoid facing his incompetence or indifference to the patient
7. when it reinforces the patient's pathological patterns of defense through an untimely attack or inappropriate gratification
8. when it increases the patient's need for active intervention or gratification by the therapist
9. when it obstructs the possibility for the patient to eventually leave the therapist
10. when it pushes the patient into action with which he cannot cope or which is detrimental to him.
11. when it leads to identification with an unhealthy aspect of the therapist.

References

1. Lieberman, M. A., Yalom, I. D., and Miles, M. B.: *Encounter Groups: First Facts.* Basic Books, New York, 1973, p. 422–423.

2. Carkhuff, R. R., and Berenson, B. G.: *Beyond Counseling and Therapy.* Holt, Rinehart and Winston, New York, 1967, p. 29.

3. Weiner, M. F.: In defense of the therapist. *Psychosomatics* 10:156–158, 1969.

4. Kubie, L. S.: The destructive potential of humor in psychotherapy. *Am. J. Psychiatry.* 127:861–866, 1971.

5. Weiner, M. F.: The psychotherapeutic impasse, *Dis. Nerv. Sys.* 35:259–261, 1974.

6. Berne, E.: *Games People Play.* Grove Press, New York, 1964, pp. 154–157.

7. Chessick, R. D.: *Why Psychotherapists Fail.* Science House, New York, 1971, p. 114.

8. Kardener, S. H., Fuller, M., and Mensh, I. N.: A survey of physicians' attitudes and practices regarding erotic and nonerotic contact with patients. *Am. J. Psychiatry* 130:1077–1081, 1973.

9. Chesler, P.: *Women and Madness.* Doubleday, New York, 1971.

10. Shepard, M.: *The Love Treatment.* Paperback Library, New York, 1971.

11. Dahlberg, C. C.: Sexual contact between patient and therapist, *J. Contemp. Psychoanal.* 6:107–124, 1969–1970.

12. Perls, F.: *In and Out of the Garbage Pail.* Real People Press, Lafayette, California, 1969.

13. Greenson, R. R., and Wexler, M.: The non-transference relationship in the psychoanalytic situation, *Internat. J. Psychoanal.* 50:27–39, 1969.

14. Greenson, R. R.: Beyond transference and interpretation. *Internat. J. Psychoanal.* 53:213–217, 1972.

15. Silverman, L. H.: Psychoanalytic considerations and experiential psychotherapy. *Psychother. Theor. Res. Pract.* 9:2–8, 1972.

16. Mintz, E. E.: Touch and the psychoanalytic tradition. *Psychoanal. Rev.* 56:365–376, 1969–1970.

17. Searles, H. F.: *Collected Papers on Schizophrenia and Related Subjects.* International Universities Press, New York, 1965, p. 701.

18. McDanald, E. C.: The schizoid problem—special therapeutic techniques. Address to the North Texas Psychiatric Society, March 1970.

19. Weiner, The psychotherapeutic impasse, *op. cit.*

20. McCartney, J. L.: Overt transference, *J. Sexual Res.* 2:227–237, 1966.

21. Reich, W.: *Character Analysis.* Orgone Institute Press, New York, 1949.

8

Use of Self with the Adolescent Patient

The ordinary adolescent patient is struggling to develop *character:* a fixed, reliable means of bringing into harmony the tasks presented by his internal psychological demands and the external world. Blos views character as a closed system that facilitates the creative use of human potential. Through the processes of internalization and automatization, a relatively constant internal psychological milieu is established that allows the individual to attend to the tasks of shaping his environment to best meet his needs.[1] The extent of an adolescent's character formation varies directly with his stage of development and is a stepping stone toward more complex and mature patterns. It is the developmental problem of incomplete character formation to which the therapy of adolescent patients is primarily addressed.

Before undertaking further exploration of the psychotherapy of the adolescent, I will briefly examine the developmental tasks of adolescence as they contribute to the formation of the mature personality. In the years between twelve and twenty, children begin loosening earlier bonds to parents and come to depend more on peers and on themselves. While in itself a progressive move, this process is always accompanied by some regression as the mature psychic apparatus of the adolescent attempts to rework earlier-adopted patterns of coping and defense. This normal regression poses great difficulties in terms of treatment and generally mitigates against treatment techniques encouraging regression—the adolescent himself is terrified that the babyish part of him will become the dominant aspect of his personality.

During normal adolescent maturation, unmastered conflicts or traumata do not often produce feelings of anxiety and helplessness; instead, they become encapsulated and help form character traits, such as a tendency to avoid certain kinds of stress (a negative reaction) or a tendency to master certain kinds of stress (a positive reaction). The normal adolescent developmental process also establishes a historical identity (Who am I and whence come I?) and a sexual identity.

Unlike the troubled adult, the adolescent cannot hope that treatment will restore him to his former level of adaptation. That would amount to regression. Defenses against unconscious conflict cannot be explored in many cases because the personality is growing rapidly, unevenly, and unpredictably and is operating out of a rapidly shifting biological substratum that includes profound physical and hormonal changes. As a consequence, defensive mechanisms often need reinforcement rather than investigation.

Openness with the adolescent is encouraged more than with the adult neurotic or the adult with a mild to moderate personality disorder. The justification for this is strictly empirical. Even though adolescents tolerate the therapeutic situation better when they experience the therapist as a real person rather than as a reflector of feelings, they do not deal well with indiscriminate openness. The therapist must temper his use of himself according to the unique treatment needs of each patient as well as the relationship between himself and the patient.

Type and Goal of Treatment

Because of the great developmental gulf between the immature adolescent and the nearly adult character formation of late adolescence, treatment techniques vary widely. However, there is agreement among many therapists on certain general principles in the treatment of adolescents.[2] The approach must be flexible. Orthodoxy of technique, regardless of type, seems to hamper treatment. A relatively strict psychoanalytic approach is occasionally useful,[3] but attempts at analysis of psychodynamics is generally less useful than helping the patient to deal with aspects of his current life situation: the changes associated with sexual maturation, his emotional lability, and his urges to act on or to avoid and deny his impulses. The adolescent also needs a clear view of the therapist as a helping person, sensitive to his needs, who at the same time avoids the seductive promise that he will fulfill the child's needs for nurturance, protection, etc.

Stated simply, the primary therapeutic goal for the adolescent is to increase his adaptive capacity. The regressive transference neurosis fostered by the unstructured analytic situation is ordinarily undesirable because of the adolescent's fear of the regressive urges that accompany this stage of maturation.

The only transference resistances or resistances to the development of transference analyzed are those which interfere with a positive alliance between therapist and patient; the therapist strengthens the adolescent more directly. He advises. He informs. He serves as a model of adult behavior.[4] He shows that a person need not deny or be overwhelmed by his feelings. He is able to control his behavior, conforms to social norms when necessary, and deviates when following would violate his integrity. He understand the adolescent's feelings but does not allow more freedom than the patient can tolerate.

Personality growth in adolescents is evidenced by improved reality testing, a greater capacity for delaying gratification, a decreased need for immediate discharge of instinctual drives, and reduced mobilization of maladaptive defenses.

Evocative techniques, because of their tendency to distract from reality, either through lack of structure or through a focus on the unconscious, are not commonly indicated. Ego-supportive and repressive therapies are generally more useful. Self-disclosures by the therapist can enhance the adolescent's reality contact by heightening awareness of the therapist as a person and focusing on the real behavior of the therapist with the patient, thus reducing the patient's involvement in fantasy and the emergence of material from the unconscious.

The Real Relationship between Patient and Therapist

The adolescent has an urgent need to know where he stands in relation to himself and his world. He needs to know where he stands with his therapist, for what purpose he is being interviewed, to whom the information will be given, and whose agent the therapist will be.

When the situation will allow only an evaluation, because of external circumstances or factors within the child, I make it clear that the interview is for evaluation only and indicate to whom I will give my information.

Adolescents are usually referred by parents or by school authorities. The most common adolescent defensive gambit is to claim that nothing is wrong with him, it's the school, his parents, or a mistake. In this situation, I acknowledge the child's lack of motivation, stating that he is a problem for others and ask his cooperation in obtaining information for the people who are concerned. I asked the cooperation of a sixteen-year-old girl who was unmotivated for therapy. After I obtained information useful to her parents, she returned for six sessions on the premise that she, too, might gain some useful information.

Adolescents with extremely poor judgment or impulse control must be told that the therapist reserves the right to breach the confidentiality of the relationship and to interfere actively should he deem the patient unable to cope with a dangerous life situation.

If family therapy is undertaken, the therapist is the agent of the family. If the adolescent is seen individually, the therapist indicates that he is the agent of the patient but is also responsible to the patient's parents, whom he owes periodic progress reports and whom he will advise when appropriate, without compromising the patient's confidentiality.

Miss H., a rebellious, negativistic, seventeen-year-old high school senior had complained bitterly about her parents' irrationality and expressed the wish that they deal with her more reasonably. When I told her I was in regular contact with her parents by telephone, she became angry and threatened to discontinue therapy if I continued to be in touch with them. I confronted her with the fact that I was her chief ally in dealing with her parents and that in cutting me off from contact with them, she was again placing herself at the mercy of their irrationality. She recognized the self-defeating nature of her threat and agreed that continued contact between me and her parents was in her best interest. Her decision to compromise was an important forerunner of a cooperative relationship between us, as well as between her and her parents.

Most adolescents do not wish to know what I say to their parents. If they do, I summarize the topics the parents and I have covered and the opinions expressed by both sides. When I feel it necessary, I withhold some of the information given to me and some of the suggestions I have made.

I told Miss H. that her mother had been advised to avoid her as much as possible, to keep from triggering fights. I did not reveal that I had advised her parents to abstain from helping her with college inquiries to allow her to assume responsibility for her own future rather than depending on, and then blaming, her parents. I felt that an open confrontation in this area would be taken as criticism and disapproval, which I did not feel I could risk at this stage of our relationship.

After a positive working relationship has been established, it may be appropriate for the therapist to reveal his emotional reactions to the patient.

I told Miss F., an eighteen-year-old high school senior, that I distrusted her father and feared that he might act impulsively and destructively toward her. She, too, expressed concern that he might hurt her during an outburst of rage. At this point, I told Miss F. that I was angered by her tendency to argue with me. I suggested that if her attitude angered me, she could imagine the inflammatory effect on her father, whom she admittedly felt was in constant danger of explosion. I hoped that disclosure of my reaction to her father would help support her reality testing.

When Miss. F.'s father arbitrarily decided to terminate her therapy, I shared my sense of loss with her, made some speculations about his motivation, and expressed hope that she would continue in therapy at some time in the future. Her reality testing had improved to the point that within six months, recognizing that she was alienating her friends, she was able to persuade her parents to allow her to continue in treatment with another therapist.

Ego Strength

The greater the impairment of ego function, the greater the need for persons who are interested and actively involved in attempts to help. This can be demonstrated in many ways.

A nineteen-year-old hospitalized schizophrenic boy, who had been overtly psychotic for a year, asked to terminate one of our sessions early. I respected his wish, but on the way out of his room I shook his hand, hoping to demonstrate that I still wished to be in contact with him in spite of his request to withdraw from me. In our next session, he verbalized anger with me. To his surprise, I complimented him and expressed my wish that he continue to express his feelings. He was able to talk with little regression for the full forty-five minutes of the session.

Confirmation of a patient's reality testing may be an important therapeutic adjunct.

One teen-age girl, an inpatient who had appeared to be insensitive to the feelings of others, drew her administrative doctor aside and expressed concern because he appeared depressed. He admitted that he was distressed by events in his current emotional life but went on to say that his feelings were unrelated to the patient or to his work at the hospital. The patient was appreciative of this honest interaction. The therapist's rationale for his disclosure was that she had made a move toward utilizing her empathic awareness and that it was important to her further development that she receive confirmation of the accuracy of her perception.

One sign of the defective reality testing of many adolescents is the inability to distinguish between act and fantasy. It may be useful for the therapist to acknowledge that he, too, has destructive or sexual fantasies and that fantasy can serve as a substitute gratification rather than a stimulus to action.

In dealing with adolescents, revealing one's awareness of their defective reality testing is a ticklish proposition. It is easy to slip away from neutral observation into angry accusation with some patients. It is best to suppress one's spontaneity with the exceptionally provocative patient. I tell the provocatively questioning or demanding patient, who is usually impatient for a reaction, that I need a few moments to consider my answer. When accused of calculating my answer, I reply that I am and that I owe it to him to think out my replies so that I can be helpful, not destructive.

The Nature of the Therapeutic Alliance

The ideal therapeutic alliance is between the rational, observing aspect of the therapist and the rational, observing aspect of the patient; this type of alliance is required for evocative therapy. With adolescents, the therapist must address himself to building his patient's ego sufficiently to deal with his pathological defenses, his standards and ideals, and his instinctual drives. It is easy to form a pathological alliance. For example, an unwitting smile in response to an adolescent's description of his sexual activity may foster alliance between the therapist's unexpressed instinctual drives and the instinctual drives of the adolescent.

A therapist who is strongly self-disclosing early in therapy is likely to reveal his liabilities, such as his tendency to condone impulsive action, to have a punitive attitude, or to promote rationalization. Having tipped his hand in this manner, he makes himself an easy mark for manipulation as therapy progresses.

One may attempt to seduce a patient into an attitude of trust by siding with his behavior against his parents or by agreeing with his perceptions. The danger of such seductions with the adolescent patient is that the therapist may place himself in the position of a parent-surrogate, in which role he continues to encourage the child to be gratified through, rebel against, or submit to a parent rather than mature and become responsible for himself.

A seventeen-year-old school-phobic girl said with much feeling that her therapy group's vigorous attacks were destroying her self-esteem, and that if she were to survive emotionally, she would need to leave the group. She said that if she were to heed the group members' wish that she stay and face herself, she would feel that she had given in, and this would enhance her feelings of helplessness and hopelessness. The only way she could see herself as being potent in any way was to leave the group in defiance of everyone's wishes.

After the group members had been given a chance to express their feelings that she was important to them, the group's coleaders each expressed their regret that the only way she could see herself as not helpless was to leave the group. They indicated their personal positive feelings about her and their feeling that she was important to the group. They suggested that, instead of acting precipitously, she allow herself to return and continue to discuss her feelings with the group, maintaining the option to quit if she felt it absolutely necessary. Meanwhile, she was encouraged to express her anger toward those in the group who had hurt her feelings rather than store it up until it was so intense that she needed to drop out of the group rather than face it. She was able to weather this crisis and remained with the group as a valuable, contributing member.

It would have been easy for the cotherapists to criticize her unwillingness to face her feelings, thus siding with her self-punitive aspect. Or, the therapists could have sided with her need to feel potent by rebelling. Instead, they indicated that they valued her as a person and as an important contributor to the group interaction. While acknowledging that the final decision about staying in the group was hers, they demonstrated that they intended to deal with her in a straightforward, nonmanipulative way that showed respect for her ability to make up her own mind.

A few weeks later, another girl in the same group began to express intense discomfort in the group. She had experienced this discomfort since the beginning of her group therapy, and with angry tears said that she wasn't going to continue to tolerate the sick feeling she went through each week in the hours shortly before the group session. When asked about her negative feelings toward anyone in the group, she said she was still angry because one of the therapists had asked about her sex life during her first preparatory interview. She said that she felt she should not have been asked such questions by a stranger.

It was evident to the therapists from material that she produced during the session that she was demanding to be forced to talk about her sexual thoughts and feelings but that such an attempt would traumatize her and might precipitate her leaving the group. Instead, they encouraged her to verbalize her anger and pointed out that this was one of the few times she had ever allowed herself to express strong negative feelings. Both therapists said they would miss her were she to leave, and toward the end of the session, she said grudgingly that she guessed she'd have to come back. The coleaders emphasized that it was her decision to make, but that they wanted her to stay for her own and for the group's sake.

Again, an alliance with the punitive aspect of the patient's superego was narrowly averted, her mature ego functioning was recognized and reinforced, and her push to take action rather than face her feelings was confronted. Unfortunately, the positive alliance lasted only one session more. Although she did terminate the group, she continued individual therapy with the referring physician.

It is clear from the above examples that the therapists did not employ disclosures alone. They communicated respect and liking for each girl and confronted the issues involved, including the girls' responsibility for keeping themselves in treatment for their own welfare instead of submitting to the requirements of the adults who were presumably forcing them to attend the group or talk about painful thoughts and feelings. In one case, the patient continued with the group; in the other, her flight was only delayed.

The Patient's Feelings about the Therapist

The patient's feelings about the therapist are an important determinant of the therapist's self-disclosures.

Early in therapy, an eighteen-year-old girl pressed me to tell her that I liked her. I felt that she identified me with her parents, whom she derided, by assuming that anyone who liked her was no good himself. She also manipulated, using the formula: if you like me, you will do me a favor. I refused to tell my feelings about her. I chose instead to say that there were times when we talked that I felt good. I left the interpretation up to her.

I have told adolescents that I like them. In each of these situations, my liking for the patient was obvious, and the patient's request to know my feelings seemed an outright request to confirm their perceptions rather than a manipulation. When teen-age patients express genuine concern, I attempt to supply the information requested.

Miss G., an eighteen-year-old high school senior, wanted to know if I had ever been in therapy. When I asked her reason for wanting to know, she replied it was just curiosity. I said that I did not wish to disclose myself simply to satisfy her curiosity. Over the next few sessions, she said that she wondered if I had needed help in working toward a mature life adjustment and if I had experienced therapy as helpful. I finally agreed to tell her because she had helped me understand the relevance of her request and the potential usefulness of the information to her. I used my self-disclosure to demonstrate that one can obtain more by making an understandable request than a belligerent demand.

The disclosure of negative feelings to a patient who feels hostile toward the therapist can contribute to the disruption of the therapeutic relationship.

At a point in therapy when Miss D., a seventeen-year-old high school senior, was feeling negatively about her dependence on me, I angrily stated that her current judgments of her parents and her boyfriend were quite distorted. She was angry with her parents for discovering her all-night rendezvous with him, but she felt no anger with him for "pushing" the drugs that precipitated her into therapy in a state of near-psychosis. I suggested she might be more appropriately angry with her lover than her parents. She told me that she had previously decided that this session would be her last and that was the way she still wanted it. In spite of my opposition to her quitting and a threat that I would attempt to have her parents push her to continue with me, she was adamant and did terminate at the end of the session.

Neither my anger nor my opinion were of therapeutic value at that point. My identification with her parents was obvious, as was my anger over her "unreasonableness." This, coupled with her concern over her dependency on me, added to her determination to flee. I contacted her parents and suggested that they take no action other than to wait and watch. She still did not return and did not seek therapy elsewhere.

The Therapist's Feelings about the Patient

The adolescent ordinarily has an empathic awareness of his therapist's feelings toward him. Nevertheless, there is room for the overt expression of the therapist's feelings about the patient. The therapist may disclose certain irrational feelings to his patient as a means of working them out with the patient and establishing a better working relationship.

Holmes reported a sixteen-year-old hospitalized girl who had shown striking behavioral improvement following her therapist's suggestion that she try to be courteous, in spite of her inclination to do otherwise. After several weeks of improved behavior, she asked for pass privileges. The therapist told her he was eager to grant her request, but he felt that his eagerness was unrealistic in view of the brief duration of her improved behavior. He used this self-disclosure to acknowledge his positive response to her improvement, while following his better judgment to withhold privileges a bit longer to help separate her from the fantasy, "If you like me (or what I do) you will give me anything."[5]

Informative disclosures of how people generally feel in given situations or at a particular point in life may be manifestations of the therapist's need to be seen as knowledgeable, but such disclosures are appropriate at many points in treatment, especially when the patient feels overwhelmed. Stories of similar feelings from the therapist's own past also help patients feel less alienated.[6]

Miss G. had been in treatment with me for a year. Her initial attitude, that her parents were her problem and that only faith in God could help, had softened to the point that she could admit to provoking her parents and could use her faith to guide constructive action rather than to rationalize inaction. She wanted to date but was hampered by her inexperience. Further, she would only date boys of similar religious convictions, with whom there was a possibility of developing a lasting relationship. The notion of dating to get around socially or for companionship was out of the question.

She had noticed a classmate who appealed to her, and after much hesitation, conversed with him briefly one day at the water fountain. Afterward, she asked me if she had been overly bold—she was fearful of rejection and wanted to know what made him unwilling to approach her first. I felt she was asking for information and reassurance rather than baiting me or appealing to me as an ultimate authority. I told her that I did not feel she had been too bold and said that from what I knew of boys, and from what I could recall of my high school days, he was probably as afraid of rejection as she. She assimilated this information without difficulty and excitedly reported the following week that he had telephoned her the same evening she spoke to him at the fountain.[7]

Physical contact can be employed with adolescents as a means of expressing positive feelings, but the therapist must be alert to the possible condescension implied by an arm around the shoulder. In one institution, the hospital discharge ritual allows patients and staff to embrace the departing patient, an exception to the institution's rule of no physical contact.[8]

Summary
The adolescent's problems are best dealt with in terms of here-and-now coping with feelings and with the real world. The fundamental task of the therapist is to increase the adolescent's coping ability by reinforcing his defenses against unconscious conflict, by helping him to develop predictable responses to life situations, and by increasing his capacity for self-observation and impulse control.

The therapist can facilitate the patient's movement toward maturation through use of self-disclosures. The patient, identifying with the therapist's rationality and his coping ability, can become aware that his problems are not unique. He can learn how people operate, and by comparing his views with those of the therapist, he can increase his objectivity. Through the therapist's example, he learns that refraining from action will not cause him to be overwhelmed by his feelings and that gratification in fantasy does not lead to action.

Obviously, the therapist's openness can be used to assert his superior knowledge or self-control. But, as much as the teen-ager may complain that he is misunderstood by the adults in his world, he recognizes that differing levels of maturity and interests are barriers between them. The therapist cannot relate as an equal without making a liar or a child of himself.

References

1. Blos, P.: Character formation in adolescence. In *The Psychoanalytic Study of the Child*, Vol. 23. R. S. Eissler et al., eds. International Universities Press, New York, 1968, pp. 245–263.

2. Welsh, E.: Discussion of psychotherapy of the adolescent. In *Psychotherapy of the Adolescent*. B. H. Balser, ed. International Universities Press, New York, 1957, pp. 144–152.

3. Harley, M.: On some problems of technique in the analysis of early adolescents. In *The Psychoanalytic Study of the Child,* Vol. 25, R. S. Eissler et al., eds. International Universities Press, New York, 1970.

4. Meeks, J. E.: *The Fragile Alliance.* Williams and Wilkins, Baltimore, 1971.

5. Holmes, D. H.: *The Adolescent in Psychotherapy.* Little, Brown, Boston, 1964, p. 163.

6. Forgotson, J.: Personal communication.

7. Weiner, M. F., and King, J.: *Self-disclosure by the therapist to the adolescent patient, Adolescent Psychiatry,* Vol. 5. Jason Aronson, New York, 1977, pp. 449–459.

8. King, J.: Personal communication.

9

Use of Self with the Borderline Patient

Borderline patients are frequently insistent that the psycho-therapist abandon his professional neutrality and interact as a real person. In fact, their persuasiveness often amounts to coercion, as we will see later. Therapists, on the other hand, experience strong reaction to these patients' intense, chaotic transferences, which are highly stressful and anxiety-provoking. Many therapists resort to a defensive emotional withdrawal, which patients justifiably see as deprivation. Others attempt to gratify what seems to be a need for a palpable human relationship only to find themselves enslaved to an unproductive, pain ful relationship from which the patient does not profit, and an impasse is reached.[1]

The borderline states and the special problems in their treatment have long been recognized[2] but have only recently come to prominence in the literature on psychotherapy. Kernberg employs the term *borderline personality organization* to describe this group of psychopathological constellations, which he feels have a specific ego structure.[3] These individuals may develop transient psychotic episodes under severe emotional stress or while under the influence of alcohol or drugs. When classical psychoanalysis is attempted, the borderline patient frequently experiences a loss of reality testing in the treatment relationship and develops a transference psychosis.

The borderline patient may seek treatment for a wide variety of symptoms, which include free-floating anxiety, multiple phobias, obsessive-compulsive symptoms, conversion symptoms, dissociative reactions, hypochondriasis, sexual deviation, and paranoid or hypochondriacal trends accompanying any other symptomatic neurosis. From a structural standpoint, the borderline patient shows specific and nonspecific indications of ego weakness. The nonspecific indications are lack of anxiety tolerance, lack of impulse control, and little capacity for sublimation. In addition, there is a tendency to shift toward primary-process thinking evidenced not only by the development of a transference psychosis in classical analysis but by projective testing.

A transference psychosis can also arise very rapidly early in the course of an ego-supportive therapy.

Mrs. Q., after a brief hospitalization for depression, was referred to me for outpatient follow-up. After eight office visits, I rehospitalized her because of heightening suicidal ideation. Our sessions, almost from the beginning, were excruciatingly painful. She spent the larger part of many sessions literally cowering in fear that she would say something wrong and that I would do something to hurt her. On several occasions, she ran out of the room in tears. In spite of her fear of me, she often expressed the wish to be physically close to me. She described the experience as being like a small child, helpless to defend herself against a parent's rage. During our sessions, this feeling had all the intensity of a real confrontation between a two-year-old and an unpredictable, sadistic parent.

The specific ego weakness of the borderline patient stems from the predominance of primitive ego defense mechanisms: splitting, primitive idealization, projection (including projective identification), denial, omnipotence, and devaluation.

These patients have little capacity for realistic evaluation of others or for genuine empathy. They can adapt realistically to others as long as there is only minimal emotional involvement. They evidence poorly sublimated aggression in direct exploitiveness, unreasonable demands, and crude manipulation of others without consideration or tact. Many borderline patients give the appearance of great emotionality and affective lability. In these respects, they resemble hysterics. Closer examination shows the borderline patient to be little affected by the emotions he expresses. It is as if his feelings are an imitation of feelings observed in others, mimicked for the purpose of manipulating his interpersonal world. The patient is like a being from another planet who has learned to traffic in human emotions without ever having experienced them.

Mrs. Y. gave the appearance of anger during one therapy session. She said, "I don't like you! Doesn't it hurt you to know that?" I said it did not. She then became tearful and declared, "You don't care about me!" I asked what relationship she saw between the fact that I was not hurt by her dislike and her presumption that I did not care about her. She said, "If you care, I can hurt you." The purpose of her mock anger was to see if she had enough influence over my feelings to push me off balance. In this case, she hoped to mobilize sufficient guilt in me to make me overlook her destructive behavior with her husband.

The "as if" quality of these patients' responses makes catharsis and abreaction of little value. It is also very frustrating to the therapist who has a need for a feeling of real involvement with the patient. Dynamically, according to Searles,

> the borderline patient is one who literally lives on the borderline between autism-and-symbiosis on the one hand, and object-relatedness on the other. It is as if he were trying to have the gratifications of both modes of relatedness, without relinquishing either mode; trying in an almost literal sense, to eat his cake (i.e. the other person, or whatever ingredient of the outside world) and have it too, to make it part of him, and yet simultaneously to make it available there in the outside world also. In actuality, he gets less than his share of either kind of gratification.[4]

The borderline patient is the result of multiple developmental failures. There is insufficient development of character to enable a smooth or predictable handling of internal or external pressures. Nevertheless, the incomplete character formation may provide a defense against psychosis. The patient can regress without the development of restitutive delusions and hallucinations. The psychological developmental defects of the borderline patient are failure of adequate self-other differentiation; failure to recognize, tolerate, and master separation, loss, and loss of self-esteem; and failure to develop sufficient self-identity and self-esteem to allow relative autonomy and the capacity to maintain stable one-to-one relationships. Because of impaired reality testing and a limited capacity to tolerate painful feelings, the borderline patient is seldom a candidate for psychoanalysis.[5] The treatment goals and methods are repressive and ego supportive, *not* evocative. The therapist offers himself as the model of a thinking, feeling person. He is willing to help the patient decide upon and implement useful courses of action and directly interferes in the patient's life when the patient is involved in a situation that may have a real, tragic outcome.

Schmideberg attempts to help her borderline patients perceive her as real by deemphasizing a professional attitude during therapy sessions. With controlled spontaneity, she sometimes discusses herself or her interests.[6] McDanald uses a somewhat different approach. He asks the patient to use the analytic couch to facilitate relaxation and sits within view of the patient. When the patient seems especially fearful or out of contact, McDanald places his hand on the patient's shoulder to reinforce his physical and emotional presence.[7]

Masterson suggests a type of self-disclosure that he terms *communicative matching*— discussing with the patient from the therapist's own knowledge some aspect of a newly developed interest of the patient that indicates individuation—whether this new interest be in music, art, sports, or the stock market.[8]

Ego Structure

The ego structure of the borderline patient must be dealt with in some detail before undertaking other considerations, and an exploration of ego structure also requires delineation of the dynamic elements that help to shape the ego. Kernberg[9] feels that borderline individuals have suffered excessive frustration of their oral needs and suggests that their inordinate aggressiveness may stem from both constitutional factors and the frustration they have experienced.

The predominant ego defenses are splitting, primitive idealization, projection (including projective identification), denial, omnipotence, and devaluation. Splitting is the active keeping apart of introjections and identifications of opposite quality—the separation of loved and hated aspects of the same person—treating others and themselves as if they were "all good" or "all bad," and not as a realistic blend of frustrating and gratifying attributes. This type of splitting is a normal stage of early ego development, now used defensively.

Mrs. A.C. saw me as an ideal person, far different from her husband, whom she experienced as sadistic and depriving. In this way, she was able to split apart and avoid dealing with the frustrating part of me. When she and her husband separated, she was unable to maintain the split, came to see me as sadistic and depriving, and sought treatment with her former hospital physician, whom she then attempted to see as all good.

Primitive idealization is an exaggerated view of the therapist as all good, which protects the therapist from the patient's negative feelings. Projective identification externalizes the all bad introjects and identifications, enabling the borderline personality to feel good. The consequence of this projection is the creation of dangerous retaliatory figures against which the patient must defend. While the borderline has enough ego boundary development to distinguish between himself and others in most areas, the intensity of his need to repudiate his aggression and his general ego weakness leads to a breakdown of ego boundaries, which allows projection of aggression. This enables the patient to still identify with the person on whom he projects and binds him to that person through his attempt to control him.

Projective identification is probably an early form of projection but differs from projection in that the projected impulse does not appear alien or distant because the self remains connected to the impulse and can thereby empathize with the person on whom the projection is made. The anxiety that initiated the projection now becomes fear of the person onto whom the anxiety has been projected, and a need to keep that person from attacking develops. There is blurring of the boundary between the patient and the person on whom he projects since part of the projected impulse is still recognized within the self, leading to a chaotic fusion of self and object. Projective identification was the basis for Mrs. Q.'s transference psychosis (see above).

The type of denial employed by the borderline personality is a discounting of the relevance of his experience or of a sector of his external world. The patient is aware that, at present, his perceptions, thoughts, and feelings about himself are opposite to those he has had at other times, but this memory has no emotional relevance. At a later time, he may react to his former ego state and deny the present one—able to remember it, but unable to link the two states.

Mrs. A. C. was subject to intense, brief periods of depression that occurred when she felt slighted in any way by her husband, friends, or me. Each time, she experienced the depressive affect as never-ending and inescapable—the only relief being suicide. She invariably denied the precipitating incident and also denied her awareness that her depressions were short-lived. The latter served, initially, as a means to escalate her demands for "special" attention which attenuated after repeated working through of her own responsibility for keeping herself alive.

The borderline establishes a demanding, clinging relationship to an idealized person partly from a sense of being extraordinary and deserving of special consideration by others. The idealized person to whom the borderline clings is not treated kindly or considerately. He is treated ruthlessly and as a possession or extension of the patient. If a person fails to provide the gratification needed or expected, he is devalued and dropped because there was no capacity for love in the first place. This is well illustrated by Mrs. A. C., who dropped me precipitously when she became unable to maintain the split between me as her "all good" protector and her view of her husband as totally depriving.

The ill-defined ego boundaries of a borderline patient often give me the feeling of having just stepped into quicksand.

Mrs. Y., who an instant after saying that I am cold and ungiving and that she has no need for treatment, says that I am very important to her, and that she would like physical closeness with me in spite of the fact that it would be detrimental to her treatment. I am at once pushed out and drawn in.

Overly enthusiastic attempts to be real to the patient can be so overwhelming that the patient's aggression is destructively mobilized. Blunders of this sort are less easily reversed with the borderline patient than with the neurotic or the hospitalized, psychotic patient, since it is likely that the borderline patient will react by leaving treatment. The neurotic will react emotionally but will ordinarily stay in treatment. Hospital confinement of the psychotic patient prevents him from leaving the scene and allows the therapist time to slow his pace, reverse his course, or acknowledge and attempt to work out his mistake with the patient.

The Real Relationship between Patient and Therapist

There is general agreement that the therapist must be real to the borderline patient, but the manner in which he establishes this real relationship is controversial. Kernberg states that opening the therapist's life, values, interests, and emotions to the patient is of little, if any, help.[10] He doubts that the patient can identify with the therapist before dealing with his negative transferences and states that the development of the capacity for self-observation depends not on offering unconditional friendship but on focusing on the patient's modes of projection and introjection, his transference distortions and acting out, and on the self-observing part of the patient. He feels the therapist must be real to the extent that he directly and openly intervenes, provides structure and sets limits (sometimes including hospitalization), and refuses to regress along with the patient. What appear to be excessive dependency needs are in the patients' incapacity to depend on anyone because of the distrust and hatred of themselves and of the internalized images that are reactivated in the transference. According to Kernberg, the working through of the negative transference, the confrontation of the patients with their distrust and hatred and how it interferes with profitable dependence on the therapist, better fills their needs.

I attempt to supply enough structure to the interview and enough information about myself to minimize the patient's fantasies. My openness as a person stimulates interaction. I use the patient's reactions to determine the pace and keep the patient in a real relationship with me rather than his own fantasies. Sometimes, the first clue that one is pressing the relationship too hard is a severe disruption in the patient's life, but the patient may give earlier warnings through increasing hostility or withdrawal in the therapy sessions and in his outside life.

Mrs. F., who was experiencing a rapidly developing attachment to me, failed to appear for her regular appointment. She called the next day, apologized, and said that she had been jailed overnight for driving while intoxicated. At our next session, she told me that she had been quite intoxicated on the way to our visit. A policeman had noticed her weaving in and out of traffic and had stopped her. The officer suggested she call someone to drive her home. She defied him, continuing to drive to her appointment. He followed and arrested her. She became abusive and was jailed. At the jail, she insisted repeatedly that she had been on her way to see her psychiatrist but refused to call a lawyer to get her out. I told Mrs. F. that it looked as if we were getting too close for comfort and that she was indicating the need for greater distance between us. She reluctantly agreed, we kept the next few sessions less intensely focused on our relationship, and she became more comfortable.

The real relationship between therapist and borderline patient is tenuous for a considerable time because of the patient's annihilation anxiety, an experience considerably different from the neurotic patient's fear of abandonment. The neurotic has been able to absorb sufficient positive life experiences to take his survival for granted. He fears the loss of persons whom he recognizes as whole, real, and different from himself. The borderline patient is incapable of taking his survival as a psychological entity for granted. Once he has established meaningful contact with the therapist, separation arouses the fear of a loss of himself—an annihilation anxiety. Once the patient has lowered his barrier to the therapist, the therapist must be able to tolerate the sense of fusion necessary to the patient for the further differentiation of his ego. A premature insistence on separateness by the therapist will trigger the patient's annihilation anxiety and provoke enormous aggression designed to destroy the therapist before he arouses further anxiety.[11]

During my six-week absence from the office as a result of my heart ailment, Mrs. U., a borderline patient with whom I had worked for two years, returned to the therapist who had referred her to me. After my return to the office, she saw each of us once a week. After several months, her former therapist's insistence on discontinuing their visits overcame her resistance to working with me alone; she feared that I would die before she terminated treatment after she had readjusted to seeing me. I said that I, too, was concerned about my heart, and that I intended to take very good care of myself and to live as long as possible. In this manner, I acknowledged the reality of her fear and accepted my responsibility to both of us to maintain my health. This served to diminish her annihilation anxiety and augment our therapeutic bond.

The Nature of the Alliance

The alliance between therapist and patient is labile. At one moment there appears to be a positive bond with the healthy aspect of the patient, and at the next moment it is replaced by cool aloofness or infantile clinging. The therapist must maintain enough distance to preserve his equilibrium, while remaining close enough to be empathically aware of the patient, in terms of feelings and real dangers.

Because I felt that our alliance was basically destructive, I transferred Mrs. B. to another therapist and refused all subsequent communication with her. In spite of this, she attempted to communicate with me by my office telephone, my answering service, or by mail, each time insisting it was urgent that I see her. One day, after having been told by my answering service that I would not reply, she called me at home and reiterated that she urgently required a session with me because she was going to quit her present therapist. I refused, feeling that she would react negatively, as she had in the past. She asked if my refusal to see her meant I did not care; I said it did not. By my listening, she became more convinced that my unwillingness to work with her was the result of technical difficulties rather than her lack of worth as a person or my lack of caring. She thanked me for listening, said she would try to make it on her own for a while, and left a present with a note expressing gratitude at my office several days later.

Chessick refers to this situation as the therapist's "crucial dilemma," trying not to minister too directly to the patient's needs or adopting a too detached and analytic approach.[12] If the therapist is successful, the patient can introject the warm, inner attitude of the therapist, develop better adaptive techniques, and use a calm investigative approach to his own feelings.

Kohut believes that it is of decisive importance for the therapist to maintain some separateness from the patient. Otherwise, he loses his tie to the healthy part of the patient's psyche, thus forfeiting his therapeutic leverage.[13]

The professed positive feelings of the borderline patient toward the therapist early in the treatment relationship are usually a thin defense against intense negative feelings that are ordinarily projected onto the therapist, who is treated as cold and rejecting if he does not respond with the wholehearted warmth that the patient says he wishes.

The Patient's Feelings about the Therapist

Mrs. P. reported that for the first time in her work with a psychiatrist (she had seen several and had been hospitalized in a psychiatric facility once), she felt a sense of closeness and rapport. I said that I, too, enjoyed our rapport and that I was glad we had been able to establish a positive relationship. After several months of combined individual and group psychotherapy, she came to a group session drunk. She seemed too intoxicated to leave on her own at the end of the session. A group member and I helped her to another's car. While I held her up, she cursed me, expressed love for me, and kissed me several times. A few weeks later, on the eve of my departure for a trip, she took an overdose of tranquilizers as a conscious expression of anger over her cancelled appointment. Mrs. P.'s wish for closeness had been overstimulated, resulting in expressions of love and hate, the latter of which she acted out against herself when she felt I had deserted her.

Idealization of the therapist follows the same path. The patient's exaggeratedly positive view of the therapist's attributes serves to protect against possible attack, expected by virtue of the patient's projective identification with the therapist. More frequently, projective identification allows the patient to attack the therapist under the guise of self defense and to negate the therapist's ability to interact positively with the patient. If the therapist displays anger at the same time that the patient's suppressed and denied rage comes close to the surface, he may overburden the patient's capacity to bear his own rage, resulting in panic, flight, or violence.[14]

The Feelings of the Therapist

It is crucial that the therapist of the borderline patient first allow himself to become aware of his feelings toward his patient and reflect on their origin before verbalizing or acting on them. The therapist's emotional reactions to this type of patient may give the most meaningful understanding of the patient's central problem at the moment. The majority of the therapist's feelings toward the borderline patient are usually not countertransference, if one defines countertransference as the therapist's attempts to relive the past in the present. They are more related to the patient's rapid development of intense, chaotic transferences and the therapist's ability to deal with psychological stress and anxiety. As such, they are useful indications of the state of the therapeutic relationship.

Kernberg notes that therapists of all levels of experience may go through phases of almost masochistic submission to a patient's aggression, heightened doubts of their abilities, and intense fear of criticism by outsiders by identification with the patient's aggression, projection, and guilt.[15] It is also true that certain conflicts of the patient may reactivate old character defenses and neurotic patterns of the therapist in the therapeutic relationship, but this is a less common occurrence.

In contemplating a disclosure of his feelings to the borderline patient, the therapist must bear in mind that to this individual, words are primarily tools for manipulation. The therapist's words are to be trusted no more than his own. Since the borderline patient is at once out of contact with his feelings and in imminent danger of being flooded or propelled into action by his feelings, the therapist cannot gear his disclosures to the expressed feeling state of the patient. Rather, he must rely on his empathic perceptions. This poses the danger that the therapist will respond to his own projected feelings rather than the patient's need.

On two occasions, I have been angrily rebuffed by borderline patients for touching them on the shoulder. One time I was expressing pleasure at being reunited after a long absence. The other time, I was attempting to express concern. Both patients made it clear that I was not to fulfill my need for contact through them.

For the most part, the patient becomes aware of the therapist's feelings empathically. Sometimes, the patient will invite a disclosure by asking baldly, "Do you like me?" If the therapist chooses to respond affirmatively, the best response is brief and matter-of-fact. If the therapist deems it best to withhold, a short statement to that effect will suffice. Elaborate attempts at explanation create suspicion, but the therapist should not, on the other hand, be brusque or indifferent to the real importance of his response.

Given the proper context, the therapist can be relatively free to express his moment-to-moment feelings about the patient. Chessick believes there must be a freedom of emotional expression with the patient, which usually involves the expression of justifiable anger (in a civilized way). Later in the relationship, he feels that the expression of enthusiasm and affection are appropriate.[16]

Havens expressed negative feelings to a borderline patient who then chastised him for being sarcastic rather than directly confronting. Havens responded, "There are times when I hate you!" based on his intuitive awareness that the patient would know that he basically felt positively toward her.[17]

Winnicott finds it useful to integrate his errors into the treatment of borderline patients. Furthermore, he suggests that, at certain phases of therapy, all blocks to further progress should be considered as if they were the result of mistakes by the therapist. As the therapist becomes aware of his errors, he should discuss them with the patient rather than defend himself, thus allowing the patient to feel anger in relation to a *past* failure of the therapist rather than to suffer an inauthentic adaptation to the error, which replicates his earlier development.[18]

Masterson agrees that if the therapist has been temporarily caught up in the patient's acting out or projections, he must admit his mistakes in perception or response. The therapist will ordinarily be excused if treatment is progressing, but the patient will not forgive dishonesty or covering up.[19]

Nadelson notes that the therapist is often seen by the borderline patient as hostile. The patient deals with this projected hostility by a sadomasochistic struggle to control the therapist's aggression as a displacement of his struggle to contain his own aggression. Therapists respond in many ways, including emotional withdrawal and quiet thoughts of murder, but may eventually develop a counteridentification that stalemates therapy. The therapist must, of course, become aware of this counteridentification. He has taken the patient's impulses into himself and is now reacting as though they were his own rather than confronting the patient with his impulses.[20]

Summary

The borderline patient, while not a candidate for an evocative therapy, can benefit substantially from a combined repressive, ego-supportive approach that helps him develop a sense of individuality, an ability to tolerate unpleasant feelings, an increased capacity to distinguish between fantasy and reality, and the capacity to maintain emotional ties and personal relationships. The treatment calls for the therapist to be seen as a person by the patient, while demanding that the therapist allow himself to become real at a pace that does not stimulate the patient's feelings to the point that he hurts himself or others or terminates the therapeutic relationship.

The treatment also calls for the therapist's ability to tolerate a massive assault on his self-esteem without resorting to direct counteraggression or defensive emotional withdrawal from the patient. The therapist's emotional reactions to the patient tend to be reactions to severe psychological stress rather than countertransference, as narrowly defined, and can be useful indices of where the patient stands in the treatment relationship, if the therapist can allow himself to reflect rather than act on his feelings.

Prudent disclosure of the therapist's feelings, aspects of his life history, his personality, and his mistakes in the treatment process can all provide useful grist for the mill if properly dosed and timed. The dosage and timing are gauged empathically by the therapist. Interventions are timed so as to emphasize separateness without suggesting abandonment, the existence of feelings without a sense of being overwhelmed, the positive and negative uses of fantasy, and the concrete steps one takes to establish and maintain a positive relationship.

References

1. Weiner, M. F.: The psychotherapeutic impasse. *Dis. Nerv. Sys.* 35:259–261, 1974.

2. Deutsch, H.: Some forms of emotional disturbance and their relation to schizophrenia. *Psychoanalyt. Q.* 11:301–321, 1972.

3. Kernberg, O.: *Borderline Conditions and Pathological Narcissism.* Jason Aronson, New York, 1975.

4. Searles, H.: *Collected Papers on Schizophrenia and Related Subjects.* International Universities Press, New York, 1965, p. 640.

5. Zetzel, E.: A developmental approach to the borderline patient, *Am. J. Psychiatry.* 127:867–871, 1971.

6. Schmideberg, M.: The borderline patient. In *American Handbook of Psychiatry,* Vol. 1. S. Arieti, ed. Basic Books, New York, 1959, pp. 398–418.

7. McDanald, E. C.: The schizoid problem—special therapeutic techniques. Address to the North Texas Psychiatric Society, March 1970.

8. Masterson, J. F.: *Psychotherapy of the Borderline Adult.* Brunner/Mazel, New York, 1976, p. 103.

9. Kernberg, *op. cit.,* p. 28.

10. Ibid., p. 91.

11. Little, M.: Transference in borderline states, *Internat. J. Psychoanal.,* 47:476–485, 1966.

12. Chessick, R. D.: *How Psychotherapy Heals.* Science House, New York, 1969, p. 160.

13. Kohut, H.: *The Analysis of the Self.* International Universities Press, New York, 1971, p. 30.

14. Adler, G., and Buie, D. H.: The misuses of confrontation with borderline patients, *Internat. J. Psychoanal. Psychother.* 1:109–120, 1972.

15. Kernberg, *op. cit.,* p. 61.

16. Chessick, *op. cit.,* pp. 154–155.

17. Havens, L. L.: The existential use of the self. *Am. J. Psychiatry* 131:1–10, 1974.

18. Winnicott, D. W.: On transference. *Internat. J. Psychoanal.* 37:386–388, 1956.

19. Masterson, *op. cit.,* p. 107.

20. Nadelson, T.: Borderline rage and the therapist's response. *Am. J. Psychiatry* 134:748–751, 1977.

10.

Considerations for
Group Psychotherapy

Group therapies have many advantages over individual treatment techniques. Each type of group therapy has its own particular advantages, but the most pertinent for our discussion are the opportunities for multiple feedback, multiple identifications, and the working through of multiple transferences. Of particular importance in relation to therapist self-disclosure is the feedback of the therapist's here-and-now feelings and his greater availability as an identification model and a transference object. It is particularly useful for many patients to receive input from others who do not occupy the role of therapist, toward whom the most intense transferences tend to be directed, for it is toward the primary transference object that the most intense resistances may develop. When in a strongly resistant attitude toward the therapist, the patient who is caught up in his transference reactions may be able to listen to the reactions and interpretations of the group members, toward whom he feels more neutral.

Group therapy patients also have the opportunity to identify with the healthy aspects of persons whom they come to know as they really are, and really feel about themselves, rather than as the facades they present in public. This knowledge of people as they really are diminishes the tendency to identify with idealized aspects of others hopelessly far beyond one's reach.

There is, of course, a price to be paid for these advantages. The therapist loses a degree of contact with the individual patient, and the patients must share the therapist with others, even when occupying his attention during the group session. These aspects of group treatment can stimulate movement toward autonomy and mature cooperation but also may stimulate a sense of abandonment and trigger regression to infantile means of competing and securing attention.

Dealing with groups is a complex task. It is manifestly impossible for the therapist to note and react appropriately to each behavior of every group member, while simultaneously attempting to ascertain and deal with the group themes that require elucidation and working through. The group therapist must also deal with his inner reactions, not only to each stimulus, but to the sheer number of stimuli. In addition, he must cope with the awareness of being under the scrutiny of many eyes. He operates in a fish bowl, under the observation of those group members who are currently observing rather than interacting.

Therapists often attempt to simplify group treatment by doing individual therapy within a group (other group members serving largely as spectators) or by attempting to deal with the group as a whole. The latter method is a more effective means to maintain the therapist's incognito. It is the basis of the Tavistock method of psychoanalytic group therapy, in which the therapist avoids getting drawn into the group discussion, answering questions, or giving direct support or advice. He waits for a group theme to arise and then attempts to bring this common feeling of the group members to the surface in a process analogous to psychoanalytic interpretation.[1]

Malan and colleagues studied fifty-five patients treated by this method and found that most patients experienced their group treatment as a frustrating, depriving experience that left them with resentment toward the Tavistock Clinic. By contrast, they tended to value and remember warmth and individual attention when given by the therapist. Malan and associates concluded that the Tavistock method is not strongly effective for the average patient, with the exception of those individuals with an unusual aptitude for psychotherapy or patients prepared by a period of individual psychotherapy.[2]

In my own experience, interactions with individual group members are more effective than interventions addressed to the group as a whole. Interventions directed at the whole group are of little help in resolving resistances to self-awareness and productive interpersonal relations. Interventions aimed at individuals have impact on the person addressed and are observed and responded to by other members of the group. This provides a model of interaction and intervention that the group members can partially adopt in relation to one another. My own technique, which addresses individual group members rather than the group as a whole, also stimulates interaction among group members. My primary responsibility is to help the group members focus on their stated treatment objectives. When they are working well together, I confine my activity to listening or making summary statements. When the group bogs down, I attempt to help individual members pick up important themes rather than interpreting the resistances of the group.

Interventions with individual patients expose the therapist more than group-directed interventions; they allow the patients in the group to recognize the therapist's likes and dislikes and his reactions to certain personalities and types of behavior. Through the process of consensual validation during and after meetings, group members can come to know much about their therapist's assets, blind spots, needs, and prejudices. This is more true in relatively unstructured groups and in marathon groups, where the leader participates in an active, personal way rather than as a conductor of interpersonal encounter exercises.

Being a group leader stimulates the therapist's exhibitionistic urges and his defenses against them. The former may lead to inappropriate activity; the latter, to inappropriate passivity.

The group rather than the individual therapist is more personally vulnerable. Because he is more exposed, patients' observations are more likely to be accurate. Since he, as a group member, responds to group pressures, the therapist is tempted to tell himself or a group member, "What you say about me is true," rather than investigate the source of the patient's perception, especially if it is consensually validated by the group. In this way, the therapist is vulnerable not only to criticism but also to manipulation by patients who are aware of his need for praise, acceptance, or other kinds of input. If a group member becomes a supplier of the therapist's needs, he can emotionally blackmail the therapist to avoid confronting him while he acts out his problems in the group.

Type and Goal of Treatment

REPRESSIVE GROUPS
Repressive groups[3] are also known as guidance groups,[4] educational groups, and didactic groups. Their goal is to maintain repression of unconscious material, while emphasizing conscious learning and identification with leader-taught values and coping techniques.

Some of the most effective repressive therapies are lay-led. Alcoholics Anonymous and Recovery, Inc., are prototypes of lay-led therapy. The therapeutic process begins with the leader's disclosure of the common problem and his triumph over it. Then each person must accept the "worst" aspect of himself through identification with other group members, including the leader. Self-worth is enhanced through positive identification with the leader and the group. This makes possible a limited abandonment of denial, a shift to more constructive value judgments, and the development of new, more realistic ideals. For many persons, it is only possible to achieve a more favorable psychological equilibrium through incorporating some aspect of one who has suffered similarly. Through mutual disclosure, the person seeking help is less able to devalue himself by feeling that he is imperfect, or inferior. In order to sustain the cure, however, he must be willing to live within his new ideology.

Professionally led repressive groups ordinarily require little disclosure by the leader. The exceptions are groups in which the leader teaches patients to recognize and express feelings in the here and now. In this type of group, the leader expresses his own feelings in the here and now. This kind of educational technique, appropriate at times in all groups, is often used in psychiatric hospitals to orient patients to the role of feelings in their lives. The danger of damaging a patient or the therapeutic relationship is not great in a hospital setting because the group is an ancillary treatment modality and the complications can be worked through by the patient's primary therapist.

Other professionally led repressive groups are predischarge groups in psychiatric hospitals, job counselling groups in clinics, and groups which help the chronically mentally ill deal with daily problems of living. In these groups, while displaying warmth and interest, the therapist instructs, advises, promotes discussion of important topics, and actively questions the group members. The essential dynamic in these groups is teaching the patient to be less distracted by his inner turmoil so that he can cope with day-to-day reality.

EGO-SUPPORTIVE GROUPS
Most once-a-week group therapy operates at an ego-supportive level, in which two important therapeutic mechanisms are interpersonal feedback about events which occur in the group and identification with the therapist and other group members.

Yalom studied patients who successfully completed group psychotherapy with a number of well-trained California psychiatrists. From his study of these patients, most of whom were well-educated middle-class persons with neurotic or characterologic problems, he categorized the important elements in group treatment.[5] He proposed that the most important mechanisms in group treatment are the patient's disclosure of himself without social facade (that is, saying what one actually feels rather than what one *should* say) and the willingness to hear the reactions of other group members to these disclosures. In this interpersonal matrix, the individual becomes aware of himself as an interacting person in the here and now. He begins to experience himself as he is in daily living and risks new kinds of interpersonal behavior in the group. He realizes that the new, more adaptive behaviors are not dangerous, and with positive reinforcement from the group, he consolidates his gains and uses this insight in daily living.

Disclosure of the therapist's here-and-now feelings can be a useful form of feedback in group therapy, as it is in individual sessions. By stating his feeling reaction to the patient, the therapist can enhance the patient's awareness of his impact on others and can validate or correct the patient's perception of others' reactions.

Mrs. A. D., after several years in a therapy group, began to perceive most of the other group members as disinterested in her, or hostile and rejecting. The group leader said he did not feel hostile but noted that she responded to virtually everyone's attempts to talk to her by feeling attacked and launching hostile counterattacks. The group members whom she had most vigorously attacked followed suit over the next few sessions, declaring that, although they felt positively toward her, they had been driven away by her hostile defensiveness. She was unable at the time to assimilate a transference interpretation: that she was leaving herself out of the group just as she had rejected her mother, presuming without evidence that her dependence on her mother would not be tolerated. She was, however, able to hear the therapist's real neutrality and willingness to include her in the group.

When feedback by the therapist unnecessarily traumatizes a patient because of inappropriate dosage or timing, the damage can often be dealt with more effectively in group therapy than individual therapy. The group patient is usually protected by his peers. Almost without exception, patients in well-functioning, ongoing psychotherapy groups rally around a patient whom the leader has traumatized.

Early in a session, Mr. B. complained of the leader's ineffectiveness. Later, one of the other group members told of a woman who married largely to extricate herself from an unpleasant situation. The leader turned to Mr. B. and said casually, "Remind you of anyone?" in obvious reference to his wife. Mr. B. was visibly shaken. The therapist had, in an unkind way, brought up a crucial dilemma. In this case, the therapist's motivation was probably retribution for the earlier negative statement by Mr. B. Without directly defending him against the therapist, the group members sided with his plight and his pain, rather than siding with the therapist's sharp inference (conveyed largely by the tone of his voice) that Mr. B. was a fool for allowing his wife to take advantage of him.

No such protection exists in short-term encounter groups because there are no strong positive ties between group members. This may partially account for the high incidence of encounter group casualties in the study reported by Lieberman and associates.[6] Patients in groups are also protected against conscious or unconscious transference wooing by the therapist. The group members rapidly detect and comment on the special quality of the relationship between the therapist and the patient whose positive feelings he is courting.

On occasion, the group joins the leader in treating one member as a scapegoat. A group leader may unconsciously encourage such treatment as a means of expressing his own negative feelings. It is, of course, the responsibility of the therapist to ascertain the presence of such a destructive collusion and to deal with it constructively.

The modeling done by the group therapist is not role playing done for the benefit of the group members. The therapist does not act concerned when he feels no concern or angry when he feels no anger. The therapist does offer himself as a model of appropriate self-acceptance, who is willing to accept the responsibility for his own feelings and behavior and able to examine those aspects of his behavior which are incongruous or inappropriate to his own welfare and the welfare of the group. Role playing by the therapist is at times an effective technique, but it must be identified as such. If the therapist does not identify his conscious role playing to the group, he may come to be seen as a manipulator who cannot be trusted to mean what he says or does. While manipulation of others is sometimes imperative in human relations, it defeats one of the prime requisites of the group: being and saying what one is. Without honesty between group members, there is little likelihood of effecting change. The group cannot deal with thoughts and feelings which are unexpressed.

EVOCATIVE GROUPS

An evocative group deals with unconscious conflict and its deepest roots in the personality. Analytically oriented group therapists allow material from the unconscious to emerge through the group process and minimize their stimulation or suggestions. Other methods, like psychodrama, gestalt therapy, and the marathon technique, use active provocation by the leader to stimulate emergence of material from the unconscious. Therapists committed to the marathon group technique make the most use of self-disclosure to elicit responses from patients, [7, 8, 9,] Gestalt therapists and psychodramatists touch and role play but ordinarily disclose little about themselves in the process. As noted previously, the marathon group therapist is in a situation of great visibility. For some marathon therapists, being disclosed appears to fill a personal need and may be an important extension of the therapist's social and emotional life. Some therapists are so stultified and frustrated by the practice of psychoanalysis that they shift from what they feel is overauthoritarianism to a more egalitarian relationship.

Mintz, a conservative marathon group therapist who is trained in psychoanalysis, reveals her feelings and shares her personal experiences only insofar as she judges they will be helpful in the therapeutic situation. She is often spontaneous, but if she is bored, antagonized by a patient, or irritated with a patient, she ascertains whether or not she is merely reflecting her own personal problems before expressing herself. She shares her own emotional problems only to maintain an intimate relationship with a patient or a marathon participant. She feels free to laugh and cry, but does not ask patients to weep over her personal griefs. Although she acknowledges that there are problems in her outside life and within herself, she does not use the therapeutic relationship to solve them.[10]

Robertiello, another psychoanalyst, is at the opposite end of the spectrum. He views his group as "leaderless."

In the group I feel committed to being totally self-revealing. The people in the group know as much about my anxieties, irrationalities, helplessness, despair, sexual and interpersonal difficulties, as well as my joys and triumphs and satisfactions as I know about theirs. I also feel I must be absolutely and scrupulously honest about expressing any feelings I have during the group or about any of the members while away from them. This includes sexual, sadistic, disparaging, caring, loving—all kinds of feelings. And I do not allow myself any "cop-outs." If I am in trouble, I must and do use the group for help or support just as any other member would. In the group I do not present myself as a paternalistic self-denying do-gooder but as a person who has a stake in getting as much as he can for himself out of the group within the limits of his professional and personal responsibilities. The group takes me as a model of openness, authenticity and self-affirmation. At first I use the very instrument I wish to defeat to achieve my end—that is, group pressure to conform. The group norm is to follow me as a model and to be open, totally self-revealing, and not yielding in individuality to any one inside or outside the group, especially to me. True, this is a norm that produces a pressure to conform. However, once this pressure sets up this particular group climate for authenticity and openness and lack of conformity, then what is created is a very non-conforming group.

Members are attacked for fitting into anything outside of themselves. They are thrown back more and more to shedding their masks (or character defenses) and to getting in touch with their unique individual feelings and needs.

Robertiello observes, "We know how many people come out of analysis looking like good docile children who have decided to behave themselves and act maturely. In the process they often lose their spark and their life and their individuality." While suggesting that the therapist abdicate the role of omniscience and omnipotence and admit his human vulnerability, he does not advocate a declaration of *professional* incompetence or abdication of the leader in dealing with individual or group resistances.[11]

The Real Relationship between Therapist and Patient

The real relationship between patient and group therapist is partly determined by the context in which the patient is referred. It is tempting to refer a patient whom one dislikes or with whom one is uncomfortable to another therapist's group. The referring therapist superficially hopes that the patient's undesirable aspect will be masked, diluted, or worked through in the group. At a deeper level, the referral may be hostile or may be an attempt to avoid an uncomfortable situation. The group therapist, aware of the referral's negative aspects, is tempted to voice his negative feelings toward the referring therapist, or act them out through an unnecessarily rough evaluation interview.

"Dumping" is difficult to avoid in clinics, but it can be diminished if the group therapist insists on a report from the referring therapist and if he personally evaluates patients for treatment in his own groups. When a patient suitable for group therapy has been "dumped" on a group therapist, it may be useful for patient and therapist to share their feelings and observations about the referral. This should take place before the patient enters the group but only *after* an adequate positive one-to-one relationship has been established. The patient may feel he was referred because of a display of anger, dependency, homosexual feelings, etc., and may have concluded that such matters are not the proper subject of discussion. The group therapist must correct this misapprehension and indicate that the problem is not what the patient said but the former therapist's reaction.

At times, a therapist is tempted to place a patient to whom he reacts negatively in his own group, rather than face feelings toward the patient and work them out, request consultation, or transfer him. A negative motivation for group placement works against patient and therapist. Patients placed in groups for this reason tend to be treated as scapegoats by the group with the therapist's tacit approval. The therapist who makes a negative placement also creates a situation in which the angry, rejected patient can destroy the therapeutic potential of the group by encouraging other group members to act out their negative feelings against the therapist or by destructively acting out his own negative feelings under the guise of catharsis.

The same principle applies to the patient who is unmotivated for treatment. No matter how great the motivation of the therapist to help and no matter how eloquently it is expressed, it is no substitute for the patient's own wish to change.

Ego Strength

Groups are molded by the leader. LeBon attributes this to heightened suggestibility;[12] Freud, to incorporation of the leader as the ego ideal for the group members.[13] The ego strength of a group (its ability to develop and work out a theme, to deal with feelings, or to engage in other constructive activity) depends on the structure and direction provided by the leader.[14] A group of healthy individuals with no clear goal or clear means to a goal will flounder more than a group of hospitalized patients who are given directions and appropriate models for becoming aware of here-and-now feelings. In the initial phases of group therapy, the operational ego strength of the group varies directly with the amount of information and structure provided by the group leader.

One gives direction to a group by demonstration and instruction. Therefore, in the early stages of all therapy groups, it is best to function in a repressive or supportive style. The leader's first task is to develop cohesion and mutual acceptance. To do this, the therapist may share past experiences with beginning new groups and his feelings in the current group. Sharing of past experiences promotes cohesion by assuring the group that the therapist has been there before and that they can trust him. His sharing of feelings also promotes identification and reassures the group members that they are not alone in their discomfort, thus establishing the emotional climate of the group and holding it to discussion of feelings that are reality based or readily available to consciousness. Such repressive and ego-supportive measures are also useful when the group adds its first new members, loses its first members, and at the first vacation from the therapist. As the group matures beyond omnipotent expectations of the therapist and mutual advice giving, other kinds of therapeutic exposure become appropriate.

Mr. F.'s life was going well except for the fact that his wife was continually angry with him. I, and two female members of the group, indicated that we felt put down and put off when Mr. F. turned our approaches to him into an investigation of our motives. I said that I could see why his wife was angry with him. My disclosure also had a carom effect. It freed the anger of one of the women toward him, which he then connected with his relationship to his wife and his mother.

Before unconscious forces can productively surface, the ego strength of the individual group members must be adequate, members of the group must stabilize in relation to one another, and there must be considerable mutual support.

Another positive aspect of groups is spectator therapy, learning about one's self or life through observing others. A byproduct of the spectator aspect of group therapy is the above-illustrated carom effect, wherein an intervention or disclosure aimed at one group member has impact on others.

Group members of low ego strength are likely to overexperience the carom effect, being unable to separate themselves from the group member to whom the disclosure was addressed. They are also prone to react negatively to special positive relationships the therapist has with other group members. This may result in outbursts of jealous rage or attempts to capture the affection of the group leader by precipitating a severe life crisis or a profound regression. On the other hand, if a patient of low ego strength is valued and well accepted by his group, he is afforded a measure of protection against inappropriate disclosures that might have overwhelmed him in one-to-one therapy.

The Nature of the Alliance Between Patient and Therapist

Because roles develop and become institutionalized in the life of a group, pathological alliances between therapist and group may be perpetuated in the group setting. In groups, two polar roles demand fulfillment: the ideal group member and the deviant. The ideal group member becomes the leader-surrogate by identifying with the leader or by the leader's preference for him. The leader-surrogate's behavior tends to be unquestioned by virtue of the halo placed upon him by the group and the leader. The deviant is the patient who differs most from the group norm. He becomes the scapegoat, based on his behavior and his negative attitude toward the group leader. His behavior and attitude stimulate the group to use this member as a target for anger or criticism equally applicable to the more popular or more accepted members of the group. In the case of the "favorite patient," therapist and group collude to deny many of the patient's problems, because of the need to make him worthy of emulation. In the case of the deviant, the self-critical aspect of the patient is reinforced by the group's need to deflect tension away from the more accepted members of the group.

The tendency to act on feelings rather than express and explore them is another type of unhealthy alliance that can develop between the disclosing therapist and his group. In this situation, the therapist's disclosingness is taken as license, especially when he indicates that acting on one's feelings is of greater value than mere verbalization.

Eliciting material from the unconscious of an individual group member must be deferred until the therapist's primary alliance is with the self-observing aspect of the patient rather than with his irrational standards, instinctual drives, or pathological ego defenses. An alliance with the superego will lead to self-criticism. Allying with the instinctual drives will intensify a patient's urge to act them out. Siding with ego defenses such as rationalization, projection, or denial reinforces pathological adaptation. The following vignette provides examples of well-timed disclosures.

Mrs. H., a hysterical woman who had withheld sexual relations from her husband for six months, was habituated to a nasal spray. She carried the spray in her purse and said that she became terribly upset if she forgot it. A number of months previously, I had asked to hold the spray bottle in my hand. This produced a severe panic reaction. I returned the spray bottle and let the issue drop; but, when the group had become more stable, I raised the question of the nasal spray again by referring to an association I had previously kept to myself. I said, "When are you going to stop taking it up the nose?" This produced some tittering in the group, some knowing smiles, and ultimately led to the relinquishment of the nasal spray. Had this intervention been premature or otherwise badly timed, it would have resulted in panic or flat rejection of the statement and further reinforcement of the patient's defenses.

Holding the same woman's hand to communicate positive feelings at a later time led, during several subsequent sessions, to her touching and holding two men in the group. Another panic supervened, and she skipped the next group session. When she returned, she said that she had become very fearful of me. Her associations dealt with her parents' lack of physical contact with her and her siblings and her fear of parental retribution. The sexually stimulating aspect of the physical contact was left untouched, to be dealt with at a later session. In this series of therapeutic self-exposures, I began with the exposure of an association. As the cohesiveness of the group and the ego strength of the patient increased, I made the more provocative tactile exposure.

A self-disclosure can be useful in dealing with a specific resistance to growth.

Mr. D. had tended to feel defeated in therapy. His notion was that there are only two kinds of people—successes and failures. To him, success meant *always* successful. One is either omnipotent or impotent. Accordingly, he had felt threatened when I did not have the answer to a problem. However, when I expressed a feeling of helplessness concerning a group member in the hospital near death, he was able for the first time to accept me as human and diminish his self-torture because of his inability to become "perfect" as he had previously imagined me.

The Patients' Feelings about the Therapist

Group reactions to the therapist's use of himself are largely determined by the attitudes of influential group members. The most valued members are idealized for epitomizing the group norms. They set the emotional tone of the group. When they feel positively toward the therapist, his disclosures tend to be seen in a positive light; when negative, the group's reaction tends to be negative. The feelings of the patients who deviate most from the group norm have little effect on the group reaction to the leader's disclosures. If, however, the group strongly ridicules a patient for his reaction to the therapist, it is likely that other members share the same feelings but are eager to attribute it to someone else.

The tendency to regard the therapist as all-knowing and superpotent is perhaps greater at the beginning of group therapy than at the beginning of individual therapy. In group therapy, the magical expectations of patients may reinforce one another. The therapist can dispel unreasonable expectations by allowing the patients to disillusion themselves in the process of therapy or by disclosing his personal limitations. However, if he chooses to self-disclose, he should not disclaim his potency. Also, the therapist need not actively disillusion a patient who enters an ongoing group that is doing well. The older group members generally reduce unrealistic expectations of the therapist without active self-disclosure by him.

Groups are usually tolerant of a therapist's human failings and tend to react sympathetically to the therapist's obvious mistakes. A sophisticated group is also aware of a therapist's attempts to avoid responsibility by pleading "human error." For this reason, members of a group can protect themselves from an incompetent therapist better than patients in individual therapy, who cannot validate their reactions to the therapist.

Feeling reactions based on distorted perceptions of the therapist are readily spotted and interpreted by group members experienced in therapy. These interpretations are frequently better accepted by patients than are similar interpretations made by the therapist because there is less transference distortion between peers. In addition, the fact that other patients have gained awareness during treatment gives a patient hope that he, too, can become more aware, helps him feel less alienated, and nullifies the feeling that the therapist is "right" while he is "wrong."

The occurrence of severe transference distortions suggests a weak ego and a need for a more highly structured treatment approach with less opportunity for misinterpretation. It is not an indication for the therapist to vigorously attempt to disprove the patient's perception of him.

The Therapist's Feelings about Group Members

The therapist must be aware of group resistances as well as individual resistances. In a group resistance, members collude to avoid dealing with anxiety-provoking material. Group silences and small talk are two of the chief resistances. Early in the treatment of a group, they are best dealt with directly. A silence can be interrupted by questioning group members. Small talk can be steered to a more profitable topic. Later in therapy, the group leader can use his own reactions to deal with group resistances. He can express boredom or restlessness in response to small talk, establishing a tie to the group members who are feeling, but avoiding, discussion of their anxieties.

As in individual therapy, the therapist must assess his feelings before he discloses them. He must not only assess them in terms of potential help or harm, but must determine if they are in fact his own. In a process similar to projective identification with the borderline patient, the group therapist may find himself reflecting the values of the group rather than his own and may help the group use one of its members as a scapegoat.

It was difficult for the therapist to avoid identifying with the group's hostility toward Mrs. A. D. (p. 132), who had so strongly attacked her peers for a number of months. The therapist was finally able to return to a more positive stance as he became aware of the transference aspects of her behavior, after having felt for a period of time that he might need to ask her to leave the group because of her defensive aggressiveness. When she terminated, it was on a positive note, and she continued in individual supportive treament.

When the therapist strikes out at a patient in a damaging way and recognizes it, he owes the patient an apology. The apology is best made at the time the therapist recognizes his error. The group's reaction to the therapist's mistake and to his apology should be elicited.

In contrast to Robertiello, I feel that if the therapist completely exposes his feelings to his therapy groups, he disregards the treatment needs of his patients.[15] It is reasonable for a therapist to explain to his patients that his objectivity is impaired because of a crisis in his own life (the death or illness of a relative). On the other hand, he has no right to make the group responsible for restoring his objectivity. That is a job for a trained professional whose own personal well-being does not depend on the accuracy of his patient's perceptions and the appropriateness of his interventions.

Physical contact with group therapy patients can be used to express the therapist's feelings.[16] The danger is that the therapist may subvert the group's needs to his own need for human contact. Careful consideration by the therapist can usually establish whose need is being met. Therapists who enjoy touching usually attract patients who seek physical contact. Even then, the therapist needs to question the importance of physical contact. With some patients it is akin to the magical laying on of hands. With others, it is sublimated sexual gratification. It can also be an attempt by the therapist to draw upon the physical strength or attractiveness of the patient. The therapist should not assume that since both enjoy contact, it does not warrant investigation.

Many group therapists have moved toward physical communication, perhaps due to the heightened pull toward intimacy in small groups and the recent trend in therapeutic techniques toward highly charged emotional experiences in the here and now. The basic questions in physical communication are, "For whom am I doing this? And for what purpose?" The therapist owes it to himself and to his patient to know what physical disclosure means and to avoid subverting self-understanding by self-gratification.

Coleadership

Coleadership is a special relationship which merits special consideration. Coleadership is widely employed in a variety of group therapy approaches: the treatment of families and marital sexual dysfunction, ongoing psychotherapy groups, and marathon groups.[17] There are many cogent reasons for coleadership. Early in a therapist's career, having a knowledgeable companion eases his anxiety, facilitates observation of the group, and provides a valuable educational experience. Older therapists gravitate toward cotherapy for other reasons. Psychotherapy is a lonely profession, as frustrating to the therapist as to the patient, but the latter may often be more aware of the frustration he endures. To forestall the loneliness and ease the frustration one can have the company and assistance of another competent professional during treatment sessions and have a chance to decompress and objectify one's experiences afterward.

A coleadership relationship can be of many types: leader-follower, teacher-pupil, master-apprentice, or equal to equal. In any case, it is not the same as the therapist-patient relationship, even if one cotherapist is professionally senior to the other. It is primarily a professional relationship, in spite of the fact that the coleaders may be well acquainted or long-standing friends. In addition, it is an intimate relationship. The cotherapy team works under stress precipitated by crises in the lives of the group members, the group itself, and in the cotherapists' working relationship, Cotherapists come to know one another's strengths, shortcomings, prejudices, and preferences. Each confronts and supports the other. When the group stalls, they examine the coleadership relationship as honestly as they can. When they come into conflict, they work toward resolution rather than stalemate or mutual tolerance. The coleadership relationship also allows each therapist to make greater use of his empathy, knowing that he can be counterbalanced by his partner should he begin to project his own needs and wishes into the therapeutic situation to the detriment of the group members.

In short-term, highly structured therapies for families and sexual dysfunction, the matching of cotherapists is of less importance than in the treatment of long-term, ongoing groups.[18] There is consensus that great care must be exercised in the selection of a treatment team for a long-term group, for this is where the irrational component of each therapist is most likely to become active, and this type of treatment will need a relationship that can withstand the confrontations that are required for conflict resolution.[19] Cotherapists do best if they have common backgrounds and similar therapeutic orientations. By contrast, their effectiveness is enhanced if they have differences in personality that allow them to work in a complementary fashion.[20]

It has been argued that a male-female team is preferable to a one-sex team for ongoing group therapy because it more closely replicates the original family structure. This idea may be valid for groups of children and adolescents, but I do not believe it holds true for groups of adults. Adults have little difficulty seeing the motherly qualities of men or the fatherly aspects of women. Masters and Johnson advocate male-female cotherapy teams for the treatment of marital sexual problems with each therapist serving as the advocate of the same-sexed patients.[21]

A more cogent argument for a male-female cotherapy team is that it may facilitate the process of identification. A female therapist would seem to be a more appropriate identification model for a female patient than would a male therapist, and vice versa. Seeing the therapists interchange roles during the course of the group might also be a useful way to cut through certain role stereotypes, for example, women are nurturing, while men are authoritarian; or women are totally accepting, while men demand certain standards of behavior as prerequisites to acceptance.

Coleadership is most useful for the novice therapist, who makes his initial entry into the field of group therapy in the company of a more experienced person in the same profession. If the senior coleader is regarded as belonging to an inferior profession there is much potential for unnecessary conflict.[22] In my opinion, the best coleader for a novice is a more experienced person in his own profession. An experienced therapist who is comfortable with his own professional identity can deal more effectively with a cotherapist from another discipline. When paired with an experienced person, the novice's anxiety is lowered because he feels less responsible and less vulnerable. As a consequence, he is less defensive, is better able to make rational judgments, and is more willing to take the risks in committing himself that will enable him to learn. His learning is further facilitated if the cotherapy team makes use of a supervisor who deals with the vicissitudes of the cotherapy relationship as well as the group's problems.

Coleadership offers the therapist an opportunity for further personal and professional growth. He can be helped by his coleader toward an awareness of his emotional blind spots and his professional strengths and weaknesses. More experienced therapists find, just as do novices, that they are more relaxed and, consequently, more emotionally available to themselves and the group. This considerably reduces the strain of the working day and allows the therapist more energy for the after-hours activities that are necessary to counterbalance the frustrations of his day.

There are also drawbacks to cotherapy. The coleaders must provide adequate time to confer after each group session. They must discuss with each other the entry of new group members and agree on the treatment approach and timing of every new person's entry into the group. They must be willing to cooperate at many levels, which some individuals experience as a drain, especially those therapists who have difficulty with equal relationships and tend to dominate or be dominated, or at least feel dominated and obliged to rebel against the imagined oppression. A cotherapist is also one more person with whom one has to contend. Each may stimulate the immature aspect of the other with resultant competition for the favor of group members or expression of hostile feelings of one group leader toward the other through the medium of the group.[23] Cotherapists may also regress to a state of inappropriate dependence on one another, which in turn stultifies the development of autonomy in group members.

Having considered some of the advantages and disadvantages of cotherapy from the standpoint of the therapists, I will view cotherapy from the standpoint of the group members. The presence of more than one therapist allows the possibility of another constructive identification, especially if there is an aspect of the personality of one of the therapists that blocks positive identification for some group members. Even if useful identification with one therapist is not blocked, each personality is limited in what he has to offer for identification. The more the number of available healthy identification models, the more the group members have to pick and choose from.

While some identifications with a therapist are constructive changes in a positive direction, others are transient identifications with the therapist as a dangerous aggressor and serve to defend against pain anticipated from exposure to, or conflict with, him. These defensive identifications are usually based on transference-distorted perceptions of the therapist. Other identifications may be inappropriate incorporations of the therapist as a whole; this occurs in highly suggestible individuals or persons with poor ego boundaries. These incorporations can prevent the patient from developing his own assets and coping mechanisms, relying instead on mechanisms that integrate poorly with his own personality. The therapist with whom a patient identifies defensively or whom the patient inappropriately incorporates has difficulty seeing the nonuseful or defensive nature of these reactions. After all, they reflect aspects of himself that he may value. The coleader is in an ideal position to detect the defensive or inappropriate quality of these identifications. He can help his colleague to become aware of the ways he is fostering these antitherapeutic identifications and can help point them out to the patient.

Group members can identify not only with the personality attributes of the cotherapists but with aspects of their relationship to one another. The cotherapists' relationship can be a model for appropriate dependency, conflict resolution, and cooperation that can be applied by group members to their own interpersonal relations.

Recent research suggests the type of cotherapist interaction that may provide the healthiest model for identification. Based on a study of thirty-three healthy families, Lewis et al. summarized the qualities that seemed important in family competence. The families were open to new ideas. Leadership was shared, with nearly equal power invested in both parents. There was a parental coalition (rather than parent-child) that worked well. True negotiation existed, with all family members participating. Family members perceived themselves and others without obvious distortion. Each family member had a high degree of autonomy, with little invasion by others. Individuals took responsibility for their own behavior. Family members expressed themselves, were receptive to others, and conveyed a positive empathic feeling tone in which conflict was quickly resolved.[24]

All of these qualities seem highly desirable in a cotherapy relationship and contrast markedly with the attributes of families in which one or more children was mentally ill or had a severe personality disorder. These latter families were highly dysfunctional. They were impermeable to new ideas. Parents ordinarily rendered each other impotent in decision making. Roles were rigid and stereotyped. There were parent-child coalitions; negotiation was virtually absent; severe distortions of perception occurred and were consensually validated within the family. There was little autonomy, much invasiveness and blaming, little open expression of feelings, a strong tendency to regard people as malevolent, and little ability to resolve conflict.

Beavers has equated the closed-system, highly-stereotyped dysfunctional family with rigid systems of conceptualizing and treating emotional disorder and makes a plea for psychotherapists to operate with the same openness to new ideas from patients, and the same willingness to share power and to enter into true negotiations as occurs in healthy families, thus acknowledging the potency of patients as people.[25] The same applies to the cotherapy relationship.

In addition to enhancing the opportunity for identification, a coleader makes it possible to work out more transferences than can a single therapist. Transferences are stimulated by some real aspect of the therapist. Each therapist, because of the limitations of his personality, can arouse only a few of the possible transference reactions for any given patient. The differences in the coleader's personality and style are bound to evoke different transferences, allowing greater access to the group members' unconscious.

The presence of two leaders can split the transference so that formerly unavailable or inexpressible thoughts can be dealt with openly. Patients frequently refuse to recognize or deal with their negative feelings toward a single therapist for fear of losing his support. When there are two therapists, the patient can maintain his positive ties with one while feeling and expressing the entire range of his negative feelings toward the other.

There are also disadvantages from the patients' point of view, especially if the cotherapists have widely divergent techniques or points of view. It is very easy for patients to get caught up in a defensive struggle over who is right rather than getting about the business of examining themselves in the light of the two divergent views or techniques. Unresolved problems in communication and cooperation between the co-leaders can significantly undermine group members' hopes of resolving their own interpersonal tensions. The experience of being used by one leader to express negative feelings toward the other may recapitulate patients' earlier experiences in a way that stifles growth and reaffirms the conviction that interpersonal relations must be managed by covert manipulation rather than direct confrontation or cooperation.

The relationship between cotherapists calls for more self-disclosure than the ordinary therapist-patient relationship. Each must know enough about the other to enable realistic trust and to suggest the probability of maintaining a positive, ongoing relationship. Knowing each other's reputation or knowing one another socially is not enough. Close friendship may be detrimental, as the honest reactions of one therapist to the other may be suppressed for the sake of maintaining needed emotional supplies from the other. There must be several preliminary conferences in which each prospective cotherapist discusses his theoretical orientation, his goals for the projected group, and his degree of commitment to the project. There must also be exploration of each other's areas of difficulty in dealing with patients, as well as the areas in which each considers himself to be strong. What one knows of his own style, whether it be confronting, nondirective, or gimmicky, must also be shared. The cotherapy team should agree to joint supervision or consultation should seemingly irreconcilable problems arise. There needs to be agreement about the rules for the group, including payment arrangements, extragroup contact between group members, the confidentiality of the sessions, and the policy regarding absences and termination. There should also be mutual agreement about prospective new members.

In their pregroup and postgroup sessions, the cotherapists review not only their reactions to the group members but to each other. In this way, the irrational elements of the cotherapy relationship can be brought to the fore and not acted out in the group.

A male coleader felt it imperative that he protect his "weaker" female coleader from the anger of an adolescent group. In joint supervision, it became clear that his perception of his coleader's fragility was incorrect and served to protect and augment his sense of potency. The obvious consequence for the group, had the problem not been aired and resolved, would have been the establishment of a group norm of masculine potency and feminine helplessness.

It is probably not necessary that coleaders know a great deal about each other's early life. It is urgent that they have some understanding of each other's major values in life, the current reality problems that impinge upon their working relationship, and an overall feeling for each other's personality. They must be willing to compliment and criticize each other. Neither can afford to regard the other as a neutral therapeutic instrument. As in the therapeutic relationship, there must be some gratification of ordinary object needs to make the relationship worth continuing. An absence of emotional reaction to one another suggests that important elements in the relationship are being glossed over and that crucial elements in the group itself are not being faced. On the other hand, the development of intense affective reactions, whether they be loving or angry, suggests the operation of factors outside the real relationship between the cotherapists and calls for an appraisal of the unconscious forces in operation. Transferences may be in operation, as well as displacements from each other's daily life. If unable to identify and work through the obvious areas of irrationality in their relationship, they can make use of several means to clarify matters. Group members can be asked to comment on their perception of the cotherapist relationship, audio or video tapes can be reviewed after sessions, or outside consultation may be sought.

Cotherapists reveal more of themselves to group members than do individual leaders of a group. They reveal not only their style of relating to different personalities and problems within the group but also their style of relating to peers and emotionally important persons. Because cotherapists tend to relax their defenses more than the solo therapist, they may also reveal more about themselves as people, relying on their companion therapist to help keep them from exploiting the group for their own personal needs.

Group members develop feelings about the therapists' having a special relationship with one another that cannot be obtained by themselves. This can restimulate acting upon strivings from all levels of psychosexual development. Oedipal strivings may be acted out by attempts to alienate the therapists from one another. Or the same oedipal wishes may be dealt with by praising the positive aspects of the coleaders' relationship as a means to deny the underlying wish to separate them. Individuals struggling with residuals of the anal stage may imagine that their words and acts govern the fate of the cotherapy relationship, that they are responsible for the coleaders' good and bad feelings about one another. Oral strivings may be acted upon in much the same way as oedipal residuals. In addition, a group member may make undisguised efforts to capture the full attention of one or both of the therapists, seeming not to notice the other group members.

Feelings of envy and rivalry with the coleaders are even more intensely stimulated by obvious affection of the coleaders for one another. Yalom advises that a newly married couple refrain from working as cotherapists with ongoing groups because of the enormous potential strain on the relationship. Once the marital relationship is firmly cemented, he sees no contraindication.[26] Married cotherapists frequently work with couples in the treatment of marital sexual dysfunction. In these small groups of two, there have been no reports of the transference difficulties that occur in ongoing, unstructured groups. The highly structured format and the relative briefness of the treatment probably account for the diminished difficulty with transference-based resistances to treatment.

Patients can become confused by differing therapeutic styles. If one cotherapist is more open, patients can assume that the other does not trust the group members or that he has something to hide. On the other hand, the more disclosing therapist may be seen as more vulnerable and in need of protection by the group. In order to uncover these issues, it is important that the cotherapists periodically raise questions about themselves and their interaction as perceived by the group members.

Summary

The group therapist operates from a relatively exposed position that can be useful in repressive and ego-supportive techniques. Although advocated by several analytically trained therapists, personal openness seems less useful in evocative groups.

The group therapist is more personally vulnerable than the individual psychotherapist. He is under the scrutiny of a group of people who can observe him interacting with others and is subject to the pressure of group consensus.

The group therapy situation, by virtue of the greater visibility of the therapist and the greater number of stimuli with which he must cope, creates tension between the therapist's need for, and defenses against, self-display. Some individuals choose to become group therapists because of their need for stimulation and self-display. Other therapists use personal openness to press the group to help them maintain their own emotional well-being.

Group patients are better able than individual patients to protect themselves against the foibles of their therapist, although it is possible to form pathological alliances with groups, just as one can with individual patients. Patients can be turned against one another to displace their negative feelings away from the therapist, just as an individual patient's hostility can be turned toward himself to protect the therapist's feelings.

The impact of the therapist's disclosures on group members depends on the context in which they are referred, the developmental stage of the group, the ego strength of the individual group members, and the feeling tone of the group toward the therapist. The therapist's disclosures may place some patients in a position of leadership in the group and enhance their acceptance. They may also result in the use of others as scapegoats, especially those who have been "dumped" into the group by the therapist or another referral source. Problems resulting from a negative placement of group members need to be worked out before a patient enters the group.

Physical contact is commonly used by group therapists to convey feelings but may detract from the group's therapeutic goal by turning the group away from constructive self-awareness and toward self-indulgence.

Coleadership has many positive and negative aspects. It is an excellent training modality for the beginning therapist. It provides the mature therapist with peer supervision and the opportunity for further personal growth, and it enables therapists at all levels of experience to be themselves under the watchful eye of an observing colleague. Patients receive greater input and have greater opportunity for identification and for working through multiple transferences. On the negative side, the use of a coleader introduces another variable into an already complex situation. An unhealthy relationship between coleaders can undermine the group and reinforce pathological identifications and patterns of interaction. To forestall such difficulties, there must be care in the selection of coleaders, and there must be open communication between them. Transferences and misunderstandings are bound to arise. Their personal integrity and their professional relationship must be strong enough to allow them to resolve such issues as they arise.

References

1. Ezriel, H.: Psychoanalytic group therapy. In *Group Therapy 1973.* L. R. Wolberg and E. K. Schwartz, eds. New York, Intercontinental Medical Book Corp., 1973.

2. Malan, D. H., Balfour, F. H. G., Hood, V. G., and Shotter, A. M. N.: Group psychotherapy, a long term follow-up study. *Arch. Gen. Psychiatry* 33:1303–1315, 1976.

3. Weiner, M. F.: Levels of intervention in group psychotherapy. *Group Process* 3:67–81, 1970–1971.

4. Krasner, J., Winick, C., Weiner, M. F., and Foulkes, S. H.: *Practicum of Group Psychotherapy.* Harper & Row, New York, 1974.

5. Yalom, I. D.: *The Theory and Practice of Group Psychotherapy,* 2nd Ed. Basic Books, New York, 1975.

6. Lieberman, M. A., Yalom, I. D., and Miles, M. D.: *Encounter Groups: First Facts.* Basic Books, New York, 1973.

7. Rachman, A. W.: Marathon group psychotherapy: its origins, significance and direction. *J. Group Psychoanal. Process* 2:57–74, 1969–1970.

8. Kovan, R. A.: Resistance of the marathon facilitator to becoming an intimate member of the group. *Psychosomatics* 9:286–288, 1968.

9. Gendzel, I. B.: Marathon group therapy and nonverbal methods. *Am. J. Psychiatry* 127:286–290, 1970.

10. Mintz, E. E.: *Marathon Groups: Reality and Symbol.* Appleton-Century-Crofts, New York, 1971.

11. Robertiello, R. C.: The leader in a "leaderless" group. *Psychother. Theor. Res. Prac.* 9:259–262, 1972.

12. LeBon, G.: *The Crowd.* Benn, London, 1952.

13. Freud, S.: Group psychology and the analysis of the ego. In *Standard Edition of the Complete Psychological Works of Sigmund Freud,* Vol. 18, Hogarth, London, p. 57, 1921.

14. Weiner, M. F.: Group therapy. *JAMA* 234:1181–1182, 1975.

15. Weiner, M. F.: In defense of the therapist. *Psychosomatics* 10:156–158, 1969.

16. Durkin, H. E., O'Hearne, J. J., Spotnitz, H., Munzer, J., and Glatzer, H. T.: Symposium: To touch or not to touch. *Internat. J. Group Psychother.* 22:444–470, 1972.

17. Rosenbaum, M.: Co-therapy. In *Comprehensive Group Psychotherapy.* H. E. Kaplan and B. J. Sadock, eds. Baltimore, Williams & Wilkins, 1971.

18. Yalom, *op. cit.,* pp. 420–424.

19. McGee, T. F., and Schuman, B. N.: The nature of the cotherapy relationship. *Internat. J. Group Psychother.* 20:25–36, 1970.

20. Davis, F. B., and Lohr, N. E.: Special problems with the use of cotherapists in group psychotherapy, *Internat. J. Group Psychother.* 21:143–149, 1971.

21. Masters, W. H., and Johnson, V.: *Human Sexual Inadequacy.* Little, Brown, Boston, 1970.

22. Krasner et al., *op. cit.,* p. 38.

23. Kadis, A. L., and Markowitz, M.: Countertransferences between cotherapists in a couples psychotherapy group. In *Group Therapy: 1973.* L. R. Wolberg and E. K. Schwartz, eds. Intercontinental Medical Book Corp., New York, 1973.

24. Lewis, J. M., Beavers, W. R., Gosset, J. T., and Phillips, V. A.: *No Single Thread: A Study of Health Families,* Brunner/Mazel, New York, 1976.

25. Beavers, W. H.: *Psychotherapy and Growth,* Brunner/Mazel, New York, 1977.

26. Yalom, *op. cit.,* p. 421.

11.

Countertransference and Therapist Disclosure

The degree and content of therapist self-disclosure is strongly influenced by unconscious factors. There are many unconscious forces operating in the therapist, including unconscious emotional reactions to the patient, unconscious values, unconscious displacements from his daily life, and countertransference. A self-disclosure by the therapist or a change in his pattern of disclosures, including his overall level of disclosingness, can point to the operation of one or more of these factors. Of the factors mentioned, countertransference is the most difficult to recognize and, therefore, has the greatest potential for disrupting the therapeutic situation. Paradoxically, recognition of countertransference triggers in the patient and his behavior can be useful to further the patient's understanding of himself. The role of the therapist's emotional reactions, his values, and displacements from his daily life have been dealt with above. This chapter deals primarily with recognizing the effect of countertransference on self-disclosure, the impact of countertransference-based disclosures on therapy, and appropriate measures for working out the consequences of countertransference-based behavior by the therapist.

Countertransference is by definition a distraction from the main goal of psychotherapy: self-awareness for the patient. Strictly defined, it is the therapist's *unconscious* attempt to relive or master some aspect of his earlier life in the relationship with his patient, instead of becoming aware of these residuals of his infantile strivings and conflicts. It is exactly equivalent to transference in the patient.[1] Countertransference, strictly defined, does not refer to conscious or preconscious attitudes or prejudices of the therapist. It refers to stereotyped emotional reactions and behaviors toward the patient that are triggered, like transference, by some real aspect of the patient or the patient-therapist relationship. Countertransference enables the therapist's ego to maintain *inappropriate* repression and other pathological defenses toward his unconscious mental life, while simultaneously allowing partial gratification of unrecognized impulses.

As stated above, countertransference is only one of many aspects of the therapist that constitute potential distractions from therapy. The therapist's character, for example, can be a significant obstacle. Certain character traits, whether they be greed, aggressiveness, passivity, or other qualities may negatively affect certain patients. The therapist's ability to understand the patient's communications is another potential problem, especially when the therapist is working in a second language or dealing with a patient from a vastly different culture. We must also bear in mind, as emphasized in chapter 9, that countertransference and other unconsciously determined reactions of the therapist must be differentiated from reactions, whether appropriate or inappropriate in degree, to extraordinarily provocative and frustrating patients. By this means, the therapist may be enabled to diagnose a borderline personality organization.

Countertransference is inevitable in any long-term therapy, even in the hands of the most self-aware therapist. Infantile strivings and conflicts are never totally laid to rest. They are merely diminished in intensity, less threatening to the ego, more easily brought to conscious awareness, and more easily controlled.

Countertransference most commonly manifests by a departure from the therapist's usual attitude or behavior toward a particular patient, or by a deviation from the therapist's general attitude toward patients in a particular case. Langs takes the extreme position that virtually every technical error by an adequately trained, experienced therapist is based on countertransference, but he uses the term broadly to include all irrational responses of the therapist to the patient.[2] Certainly, a significant lapse in technique should be investigated for the presence of countertransference factors, but the issue is greatly complicated in the case of the inexperienced therapist who has not yet crystallized out a basic approach to patients in general or to particular categories of clinical problems. For the novice, the manifestations of countertransference will differ in this respect from the experienced therapist. Overt countertransference reactions *are* technical errors, in that they reflect intrusion of the therapist's unconscious into the patient's therapy, thus subordinating the patient's treatment needs to the therapist's defensive operations.

There are many clues to significant countertransference problems. Attempting therapy under unusual circumstances may suggest that the therapist is responding to his own needs more than to those of his patient. These might include an offer to see a patient for no fee or away from the therapist's office, or for the therapist to agree to work with a person with whom he has an existing personal, professional, or business relationship, as well as the therapist's tendency to be late, miss, change the length of sessions, or change appointment times inordinately often. I find that relegating patients' appointments to my secretary can be a clue about my unconscious reactions to a patient. Making the next appointment myself may indicate that the patient's return has special significance to me. If I too readily shunt him to my secretary, it may suggest some discomfort on my part in the relationship.

Marked changes in the therapist's ordinary technique are another obvious signal not only that he may be dealing with a special problem in the patient but that the patient may have some special unconscious significance for him. For example, the therapist who ordinarily maintains a neutral stance may feel impelled to disclose himself to a particular patient without obvious need on the patient's part. Such gratuitous disclosures almost invariably point to the operation of unconscious factors in the therapist, some of which may be countertransference-based. Other clues to countertransference may be preoccupation with the patient away from the therapy hour, including repetitive dreams about the patient,[3] sexual or hostile fantasies about the patient, seductive or quarrelsome behavior with him, and a heightening of the therapist's defensiveness, manifested by a need to reiterate and defend his interventions with the patient.

Countertransference can be employed constructively if the therapist can recognize it and discover the part of the patient that stimulated its appearance. As stated previously, it most commonly takes the form of technical errors or inappropriate attitudes of the therapist. In either case, it is best treated with the patient as a technical error. After acknowledging his inappropriate behavior, the therapist can use the patient's subsequent associations and responses to reconstruct the situation as it really occurred and to understand what its meaning is to the patient. The therapist who is willing to be truthful in this way also establishes a potentially useful identification model of courage, honesty, and willingness to accept responsibility for awareness and control of his own actions. He also indicates, by having made the error, that he is not superhuman but an ordinary human being who must continue to make conscious efforts to be self-aware.

Overt manifestations of countertransference should be controlled and limited. They should be used to understand and work out the patient's emotional problems, be resolved through the therapist's own introspection, and worked through with the patient without burdening the patient with the therapist's problems.

Self-disclosures, or even failure to disclose at appropriate moments, can be symptomatic of countertransference difficulties.

I maintained an unusually rigid degree of neutrality with Mr. I., who had come to me because of his wife's awareness that he had sexually molested her child. She and the child had moved out of the house, and she had instituted divorce proceedings. His primary motivation for psychiatric consultation was to prevent a divorce. He saw no further problem in terms of the relationship between himself and the child. He was certain that he would never again make sexual advances toward her, in spite of the fact that he had frequently initiated sexual intimacy with her over a period of two years and that the child had terminated the sexual aspect of their relationship, not he. In fact, he persisted in entering the child's bedroom each morning, insisting on rubbing her back, until his wife finally suspected he was molesting her and obtained the story from the child. I had little difficulty seeing that, on one level, I was passively acting out my anger at a man for whom therapy was only a means to manipulate his family situation, who was unwilling to face the destructive way in which he had been meeting his own needs, and who was also unwilling to work on the problem within himself. In retrospect, however, it occurred to me that I was rejecting that part of me (which I projected onto him) that could conceive of sexual intimacy with a child.

A gratuitous exposure, for which there is no obvious therapeutic indication, is similarly a countertransference manifestation. My comment about my religious affiliation to Mr. E. (see chapter 2) was out of context in the therapeutic relationship. At the moment of the disclosure, I had no conscious wish to hurt or shock him. There is little doubt, having been aware of his background, that I was aware of the potential impact of such a disclosure. I unconsciously asserted, "I am not like him," but the issue on which I was attempting to separate myself from him was not religious or political, but sexual. We were able to make some headway in therapy afterward, but he and I eventually stalled and agreed that he might fare better with a therapist who was Christian, like himself, avoiding the underlying issue that I had unconsciously emphasized our dissimilarity to forestall dealing with the aspects of myself that were uncomfortably close to his sexual problems.

Self-disclosures that are acts of aggression against the patient, whether overtly hostile or disguised as kidding or humorous teasing, are frequent manifestations of countertransference. I do not believe my sarcasm with Mrs. E., who complained about the lack of freedom in my office, was countertransference-based. I think it was direct counteraggression in response to her attack on me. My sarcasm with Mrs. U. reflected the anger I felt at being unable to make a dent in her wooden facade. Disclosure of my reactions to Mrs. F.'s friend probably had a partial countertransference basis in my wishes to advance myself socially, stemming from earlier competitive urges.

The disclosure of my sexual attraction to some patients, while affirming their sexual attractiveness, was in some cases an acting out of countertransference. The deleterious effect of several disclosures of this sort was an intensification of the patients' attention to our relationship and a concentration of their energy on obtaining further gratification from me instead of further insight into their problems. Simply telling Mrs. B. that I liked her and holding her hand were sufficient to greatly impair her ability to deal directly with negative feelings toward me. Instead, she acted them out by getting drunk, calling in the middle of the night to express her love, and attempting to undo her intrusion into my privacy by prolonged, profuse apologies that kept me awake even longer.

Since countertransference-based disclosures relate only tangentially to the patient, their effects are frequently antitherapeutic in the sense that they delay work on the patient and provide material for the patient to work through beyond the problems generated by his ordinary life situation and his own pathology. Occasionally, the countertransference reaction to the patient will lead to a valuable insight about the patient's impact on others. There are many possible negative effects. The therapeutic alliance can be disrupted temporarily, or even permanently. The patient's self-deprecating tendencies can be augmented, or he may begin suddenly and inappropriately to act out aggressive and sexual feelings during and outside of the therapy hour. The patient may regress or experience marked worsening of his presenting symptoms. Should any of these difficulties arise in the absence of changes in the patient's other significant relationships, the therapist can assume he has made a technical error. The therapist's unawareness of the error at the time it occurred points strongly to the possibility of a countertransference basis.

Lesser degrees of negative reaction to countertransference-based disclosures include dreams or fantasies of being seduced, attacked, penetrated, harmed, or tortured.

Mr. K., who had been in treatment several years because of low self-esteem, depression, mild paranoid ideation, and difficulty maintaining social relationships, was virtually unable to tolerate the therapist's empathic smile or his attempts to recapitulate or summarize Mr. K.'s statements. Any act by the therapist other than utterly neutral explorations of his communications was met with rage. Over several years, Mr. K. became able to verbalize that he felt my interventions as feared sexual penetrations. He dealt with my smiles by asking each time if I were laughing at him and seemed able to accept my explanation that I was laughing at the irony or humor of the situation, not at him. In spite of his negative reactions to my behavior, I persisted in my attempts to nonverbally communicate empathy and to summarize his statements. Eventually, I began to understand that my persistence in the face of his rage was not a sign of dedication to duty but of the operation of countertransference factors that were perpetuating a sadomasochistic relationship similar to his relationship with his father.

If one but listens to the manifest and latent content of the patient's productions, he can glean significant clues to the presence of countertransference-based interventions. The problem for the therapist is to have sufficient ability to observe in a detached manner, to be able to consider that the patient's "distorted" perceptions of the therapist or "exaggerated" negative reactions may be entirely appropriate, when considered in the light of the patient's specific needs and vulnerabilities.

When the therapist realizes that his behavior is countertransference-based, he must strive to control and understand it. The patient's reaction should be allowed to unfold but must be adequately dealt with before it leads to destructive behavior, in the form of acting out or regression.

Miss S. reported that she was experiencing some relief from her chronic depression. At the end of the session, the therapist expressed his pleasure at her improvement by saying, "I'm glad you're feeling better." At the next session, she reported feeling worse. She volunteered that the therapist's happiness over her improvement had made her uneasy. On further questioning, she said she feared her treatment would be terminated at a point when she was not yet ready to be on her own. She recalled her family's move when she was ten, and the difficulty they had in finding a doctor who could care adequately for her diabetes. By the end of the session, it was obvious to Miss S. that the therapist had heard and understood, and there was no imminent danger of immediate termination based on the false premise that she was fully recovered.

One must take into account that the patient's "distorted" perceptions of the therapist may accurately capture what the therapist is actually acting out in the therapeutic relationship.

Mrs. A. E. told me that a friend had described a medical colleague of mine as uncommonly good-looking. I responded, "He's gorgeous." In our next session, the patient returned to a concern she had expressed early in therapy—that I might be homosexual. This served as a temporary block to dealing with dream material she had reported in which there were homosexual overtones. The block was resolved by helping her see that she was dealing with her anxiety by projecting the feared part of herself onto me and by agreeing that we were talking about homosexual thoughts and feelings and not defining her as either "straight" or homosexual.

When dealing with the therapist's technical error as an error, the therapist should briefly and simply admit it and acknowledge that he is seeking the source of the error within himself, but he need not go on to say what he discovers. Neither of the above incidents was treated as an error by the therapist, but both patients were allowed to react fully, with the therapist making appropriate corrective remarks.

Using the therapist's countertransference-based slip as the stimulus, the patient's response is evaluated and interpreted in terms of his own needs and problems. The therapist's error is not a license for the patient to act out or regress. Many patients will use the therapist's errors to sanction disruptive behavior or to rationalize their own pathology, but the therapist's realistic sense of responsibility should not lead him to feel totally responsible for the patient's behavior. If he does, he sets himself up for emotional blackmail by the patient, who acts the role of helpless victim. The therapist should not deny his provocation or assume undue responsibility. Emotional growth for patient and therapist can result from investigating the patient's reaction to the therapist's inappropriate behavior, but there is also the possibility that, in times of future stress, the patient will use the incident to reinforce his defenses and resistance. The therapist should not overplay the errors he has made, nor should he reinforce the patient's sense of being misunderstood. And, of course, the therapist must recognize when the patient uses the error to disrupt therapy or to maintain his current life style and avoid change.

My disclosures to Mrs. L., while partly a conscious attempt to build rapport, also had countertransference determinants. The clues to the countertransference aspects of my behavior were my conscious dread of our sessions, my discomfort during the treatment hours, and my attitude toward her, markedly different from my usual attitude toward patients. This difference in attitude was highlighted in the therapy group, where the other patients became aware that in spite of her minimal contribution to the group, she was somehow special to me. Mrs. L. introduced my earlier disclosures into the group as technical errors. Her purpose, however, was not to work out our problems or strengthen our relationship in a healthy way but to reinforce her defensiveness and to justify acting out her anger toward me without having to deal with its roots in her unconscious mental processes. After she left therapy, the group and I discussed my irrational involvement with her and concluded that both of us were responsible for undermining her treatment; she through lack of motivation, and I through my inappropriate emotional involvement. Those in the group who had formerly envied her "specialness" to me came to appreciate my more controlled, rational involvement with them and were grateful that they had been appropriately frustrated and not inappropriately gratified.

Summary

Many unconscious factors influence the degree and content of therapist disclosure. The most difficult to recognize, to adequately manage, and to resolve are countertransferences: attempts by the therapist to relive certain aspects of his own past in the therapeutic relationship. Countertransference is inevitable because the unconscious can never become fully available to conscious scrutiny. As a result, one must heed derivative processes, such as a change in the therapist's attitude toward a patient, or the therapist's dealing with one patient in a manner markedly different from the way in which he treats other patients. One also suspects countertransference-based behavior by the therapist when the patient, in the absence of changes in other relationships, begins to have negative reactions to therapy.

Once detected, countertransference behavior by the therapist must be controlled and understood. It can be dealt with in the patient's therapy as a neutral stimulus for associations or as a technical error, whose ramifications for the patient require exploration as would any traumatic event in his life. Without assuming an unreasonable degree of blame for the consequences, or letting the therapist's misstep be construed as license for the patient to act out or disrupt the therapeutic alliance, the therapist's error is acknowledged and its consequences are worked through by a thorough examination of the patient's reactions and a change in the therapist's behavior to a more appropriate therapeutic mode.

References

1. Greenson, R. R.: *The Technique and Practice of Psychoanalysis*, Vol. I. International Universities Press, New York, 1967, p. 348.

2. Langs, R. J.: *The Technique of Psychoanalytic Psychotherapy,* Vol II. Jason Aronson, New York, 1973, p. 308.

3. Whitman, R., Kramer, M., and Baldridge, B.: Dreams about the patient. *J. Am. Psychoanalyt. Assoc.* 17:702–727, 1969.

12.

Conclusions

There is no way to entirely exclude the person of the therapist from psychotherapeutic interviews. One is disclosed to some degree in any interaction, whether one is primarily an observer or an active participant. Use of self in psychotherapy involves not only the therapist's deliberate exposure of himself as a person but also includes dealing actively with those parts of his person which inadvertently intrude into the therapeutic relationship. Some situations are inherently more disclosing of the therapist than others. Ongoing therapy groups and marathon groups most clearly expose the personality of the therapist. Patients in psychoanalysis and in highly structured therapies may see very little of the therapist as a person. In every situation, however, some aspect of the personality of the therapist comes into play and must be dealt with. Transference reactions in neurotics are triggered by some real behavior on the part of the therapist, which is related in turn to some aspect of his personality. (Intense transference reactions without apparent triggers suggest severe ego impairment.) Therapists often act out their countertransference in what they disclose or refuse to disclose. There are also issues that go beyond transference, countertransference, and their interpretation, including the need of therapist and patient for emotionally meaningful human contact during the therapy hour.

I will now readdress, in summary form, the questions that have been raised concerning use of self in psychotherapy.

1. What purpose can be served by deliberate introduction of the therapist's person into the therapeutic process?

2. How can the therapist become aware of inadvertent disclosures?
3. What are the most helpful self-disclosures?
4. How much disclosure is useful?
5. When does the therapist actively withhold his person?
6. What role does the therapist's honesty about himself play in therapist-patient transactions?
7. What are the indications and contraindications for use of self?
8. What are appropriate object-need gratifications between therapist and patient?

What Purpose Can Be Served by Deliberate Introduction of the Therapist's Person?

By introducing himself as a person into the treatment process, the therapist can reduce a patient's sense of alienation and help him recognize that although a troubled person, he is more like others than he is different from them. This is much more important for patients with severe emotional disorders that require institutionalization and withdrawal from normal forms of esteem-enhancing interactions with others.

Self-disclosures by the therapist can facilitate the opening-up process for the severely disturbed patient as he feels the therapist's liking and respect for him as a person of worth and dignity. Occasionally, a therapist can facilitate interaction between himself and his patient by a catalytic self-disclosure, such as his own self doubts in a past situation that was similar to the patient's.

Therapists' disclosures can support and validate patients' perceptions and can clarify the real relationship between therapist and patient. They can help patients become aware of their impact on others, help patients distinguish between fantasy and reality about their therapists as people, and also help patients to see that neither they nor their therapists need be omniscient or omnipotent to be potent. By revealing that he has fantasies and makes use of gratification in fantasy as a substitute for acts such as physical aggression, the therapist can help his patients distinguish between fantasy and act and recognize that a fantasy need not culminate in action.

Self-disclosures by the therapist can augment the separation-individuation aspect of psychological maturation. Allowing the patient to know that he is special through direct disclosure of feelings or by opening some special aspect of one's self to the patient sets the stage for working through a patient's feelings that he can be special to another person only if subservient to or not fully differentiated from that person. As the patient begins to realize that he and his therapist have achieved emotional closeness without compromising the patient's freedom to be himself, he begins to entertain the possibility of being himself in other meaningful relationships.

In addition, the therapist can serve as a useful model of adult behavior through his reasoned, calm approach to problems, his self-acceptance, his willingness to listen to others, and his ability to modify or defend his point of view. Cotherapists can serve as models of mature adult interaction, especially in their demonstrated ability to share, to cooperate with one another, to resolve problems between themselves, and to work as a team while respecting each other's differences in personality and therapeutic style. The extent to which personal characteristics or the type of interaction is useful as an identification model depends on many factors, including transference and the patient's ability to integrate what he has observed into the fabric of his personality. Sometimes, things just don't fit. Sometimes, a therapist literally doesn't have what it takes, and while able to give advice or help the patient achieve insight, the therapist may not be able to serve as an identification model because of the limits of his personality.

The aspects of the therapist that are perceived by the patient, whether correctly or incorrectly, serve as a nidus for transference formation. To the extent that an incorrect perception blocks the patient's progress in therapy, it needs to be corrected. If the patient becomes overwhelmed by his reactions to the personality of the therapist, the therapist must take a more neutral stance and interpret the transference instead of making further disclosures in the hope that the patient will come to see him more realistically.

In a sense, the greater the exposure of the therapist, the greater possible number of transferences that can be elicited and resolved. From another point of view, the more transferences that are simultaneously evoked, the greater confusion for both patient and therapist. This is the essential problem of cotherapy in terms of the transference. There is more opportunity for transference development and resolution but there is also an equally great opportunity to become so wrapped up in the realistic stimuli for the transference reactions that the transference aspects become lost and go uninterpreted.

How Can the Therapist Become Aware
of Inadvertent Disclosures?

Observing oneself in videotaped interviews is the best way to become aware of inadvertent disclosures. Serial interviews with a single patient show the therapist's responses to changes within the context of a single relationship. Tapes of interviews with a wide variety of patients show habitual responses to certain kinds of patients, as well as the way in which the therapist expresses certain feelings. One's first encounter with oneself on videotape is often a shock. The greatest surprise is one's nonverbal communication through mannerisms, physical responses, and tone of voice.

In group psychotherapy, the cotherapist serves a function similar to the television monitor. In postgroup sessions, coleaders point out each other's behaviorally communicated messages.

Supervision and self-observation through careful record keeping are also useful but are considerably less objective than videotape recordings or direct observation by a coleader, unless one has had considerable prior experience with self-observation through either of these objective methods or through a personal psychotherapeutic experience.

What Are the Most Helpful Disclosures?

The therapeutic effectiveness of a self-disclosure depends as much on its context and dosage as its content. An improperly timed therapist disclosure can be experienced by the patient as an inconsiderate, narcissistic display. At another time, it may be perceived as evidence of a strong empathic bond. Insistence that the patient be aware of the therapist can be a frightening, unwanted intrusion under certain circumstances. Under others, it may be a welcome relief from the patient's long-standing alienation of himself from others.

The most useful disclosures are those whose content, dosage, and timing indicate respect for the patient. Showing respect does not imply wholehearted personal involvement or total approval. It does connote serious professional involvement. Patients in therapy often see the offer of a human relationship as an additional burden. They come to treatment seeking relief from emotional suffering through concrete advice, medication, or hospitalization if they are unable to manage their own lives. In these situations, the therapist shows his respect by remaining personally neutral until the patient is willing, able, or has the need to be involved in a personal way with the therapist.

Equally useful are disclosures that help improve the patient's reality testing by correcting transference distortions and misconceptions due to misinformation or misperception, and by supplying information not previously available or usable.

Under all but the most extraordinary circumstances, patients do not require self-disclosures by the therapist to establish an empathic bond, acceptance, or trust. These attributes of the relationship are almost always communicated indirectly through the therapist's actions and attitude toward the patient. Most patients are aware that words are cheap and that actions are a more reliable indicator of feelings and of the state of a relationship.

It is useful for the therapist to communicate his understanding *if* he understands. It is important, however, that he check with the patient, perhaps by rephrasing the patient's statement in his own words, before nodding and saying, "I understand." Therapists are eager to be seen as understanding, but the appearance of understanding is no substitute for actual comprehension.

It is also useful for the therapist to state the problem areas in which he will not or cannot help. For example, he may defer to the patient's lawyer for suggestions about the mechanics of obtaining a divorce, reserving for himself the role of elucidating and examining the meaning and emotional impact of such an action. The therapist also needs to communicate his willingness to help with those problems for which the patient wishes assistance.

Disclosures must be authentic in the sense that they must be the product of the therapist's wish to share, and not a gimmick the therapist has learned in order to give the appearance of sharing. A therapist who is innately nondisclosing is wise to work within the confines of his personality rather than forcing himself into an inauthentic relationship with his patient.

How Much Disclosure is Useful?

Self-disclosingness per se is not useful. The utility of self-disclosure is determined by its appropriateness rather than its degree. Within limits, self-disclosingness in nontherapy situations stimulates self-disclosure by others. In the psychotherapeutic situation, it is not similarly effective. Patients are aware that effective treatment depends on their willingness to be open, not on the therapist's transparency to them. Only the most naive therapist feels, under ordinary circumstances, that the patient's opening up is contingent upon his degree of openness with the patient.

There is evidence, however, that if self-disclosingness is an authentic part of one's self and if it is combined with accurate empathy and unconditional positive regard, the outcome may be enhanced with hospitalized schizophrenic patients.[1] Unfortunately, it has not been possible to bear out these findings in other patient populations. It is understandable that experiencing the human qualities of the therapist may be crucial for hospitalized schizophrenics, who are actively attempting to renounce the pain of human relationships. To find a single relationship in which they are not treated as objects to be manipulated for the gratification or protection of others may be the essential, needed ray of hope to start on the road back. The neurotic and the character disordered are more likely to feel they have stumbled across yet another fool to be manipulated.

When Does the Therapist Remain Neutral?

Neutrality is the safest initial stance for the therapist. It protects the patient from the potentially harmful aspects of the therapist's personality, while protecting the therapist from manipulation by the canny patient. As the therapist comes to know the patient better, he can afford to be more open, on a selective basis. Neutrality allows the therapist the opportunity for history taking without the additional contamination of the patient's reaction to him as a person, which will certainly color the material that is produced. Under ordinary circumstances, keeping clues about oneself at a minimum will initially help the patient keep the focus on himself.

Neutrality is an important part of the treatment for certain patients. The therapist may withhold information about himself from selected patients to help them recognize transference distortions as they arise and change during the course of therapy. Some transference distortions cannot be worked through without self-disclosure by the therapist. Such was the case with the wolf man, who needed to learn that he was not Freud's favorite patient in order to deal with his anger toward his father.

Drawing on his work with chronic schizophrenics, Searles holds that neutrality is neither a luxury for the therapist nor mere self-protection from feelings. He sees the therapist's neutrality as a hard-won, difficult-to-maintain state that can be lifesaving to a patient who has been constantly intruded upon by the reactions and feelings of others.[2]

What Role Does the Therapist's Honesty about Himself Play in Therapist-Patient Transactions?

The therapist needs to be honest about his professional qualifications, the general nature and duration of the intended treatment, and what will be required of the patient. He does not owe his patient further personal information, but the therapist does owe his patient an explanation for withholding. Patients may need to be told that the therapist, like anyone else, is entitled to a degree of privacy, that he is not maliciously depriving his patient of his own life, thoughts, or feelings. But an arbitrary statement that the therapist will not discuss himself is demeaning to the patient. On the other hand, there should be a sound reason for disclosing himself to the patient. Being honest about himself may reduce some patients' anxiety. Other patients hear disclosures as self-condemnations or convenient rationalizations, and with these patients one must be circumspect.

Of extreme importance in relation to self-disclosure is that dishonesty is not the only alternative to complete honesty. There are alternatives to dishonesty, such as (1) telling only as much of the truth as is necessary, (2) telling the truth when it is most likely to be helpful, and (3) withholding information—asking a question in response to a question, changing the subject, or making an outright refusal to volunteer information. When the therapist demonstrates that the alternative to truth is *not* dishonesty, patients can free themselves from states of childish dependency and self-condemnation as liars when protecting themselves from the harmful consequences of telling the truth at the wrong time and place. For the purpose of the psychotherapeutic relationship, honesty is a tool, not a moral absolute, and certainly not always a virtue.

What Are the Indications and Contraindications for Use of Self?

The therapist should refrain from being real until he has data that suggest its probable impact. The indications and contraindications are determined by the real relationship between therapist and patient, the type of treatment employed, the state of the therapeutic alliance, the patient's ego strength, the patient's feelings about the therapist, and the therapist's feelings about the patient.

If the patient comes to the therapist strictly for evaluation, the therapist does well to remain neutral. However, it is the therapist's obligation to state if he is not the agent of the patient. If, after the evaluation, the therapist is unwilling or unable to assume the burden of treating an individual seeking therapy, he owes the patient an explanation that allows both to maintain their dignity.

Self-disclosure may be employed in repressive, ego-supportive, and evocative therapies. In repressive and supportive therapies, it provides feedback at an interpersonal level, an avenue for identification, and a distraction from unconscious processes. The therapist, however, does not relinquish his position of expertise. It must be remembered that the therapist who offers himself as a model offers his personal limitations as well as his positive attributes. In self-disclosing, the therapist must also be careful to maintain the focus of the therapeutic session on the patient. This does not obviate the occasional necessity for patient and therapist to review the attitudes of the therapist *in relation to the patient*. There is no need to extend the scope of their discussion to the therapist's other relationships unless they are commonly shared, as with the therapist's relationships to other members of a therapy group or his coleader.

In evocative therapies, the therapist must provide sufficient information about himself to adequately orient the patient and avoid the dehumanizing effect of total frustration. On the other hand, he must be careful not to present so much information about himself that he obscures material from the patient's unconscious or helps the patient rationalize his transference distortions or his acting out. Inadvertent self-disclosures stimulate the development of transferences. Deliberate disclosures may be useful in the resolution of these distortions once an adequate working alliance has been established with the rational, observing ego of the patient. The development of the capacity for noncritical, nonjudgmental self-observation is a necessity for the success of an evocative therapy. It is only after the ego has been "split" into a neutral observing portion and an interacting portion caught up in the transference that disclosures or interpretations will be useful in dissolving the transference resistances to further insight.

As a general rule in any type of therapy, the therapist should not introduce his personal reactions until a constructive working relationship has been established with the patient. This differs from the development of the observing ego described above. By a constructive working relationship, I mean rapport—the sense that therapist and patient are working together toward a mutually agreed-upon goal. A perplexed patient who is just beginning psychotherapy is relieved when the therapist is aware of his confusion and offers him a frame of reference to guide him through the early stage of their relationship. It may be damaging if the therapist responds to the patient by admitting his own perplexities, offering nothing more than his own confusion to guide the patient. Disclosing some aspect of one's self to seduce an unmotivated patient into a working relationship frequently backfires, leaving the therapist feeling naked and foolish and the patient feeling he has won a hollow victory. Only with the most regressed patients is it necessary to "loan" a bit of one's self to supply sufficient hope and energy to spark a positive interaction. A healthier patient who wants the therapist to "show and tell" is usually trying to avoid dealing honestly with his own lack of motivation for self-exploration.

The therapist must be aware of the patient's predominant intrapsychic and interpersonal defenses, level of maturity, and both the developmental tasks at which he has failed and those which he is now facing. Appropriately timed disclosures can be used to cut through the projective identification and defensive splitting of object relations employed by the borderline patient. Disclosures can be used to establish that the therapist has thoughts and feelings that differ from his adolescent patient, who wishes for and fears a return to the more nearly symbiotic relationship of earlier childhood, rather than face the uncertainties of becoming his own person. Disclosure that one's thoughts and feelings differ from those attributed to one by the patient can be useful with individuals who have difficulty seeing the therapist as an individual rather than as their projected thoughts and feelings.

The therapist must be aware of the impact of particular types of disclosures on patients with certain dynamic constellations. Disclosing feelings of friendliness to a paranoid patient may heighten his suspicions. Expression of sympathy for a severely depressed person may heighten his feelings of unworthiness. The patient must have enough ego strength to integrate disclosures that the therapist makes to him. Telling a psychotic girl who is overwhelmed with disgust at her own sexual impulses that she is attractive to the therapist may intensify her psychotic retreat.

When the therapist makes an error in treatment that is detected by the patient, it is advisable for the therapist to acknowledge his error to confirm the patient's perception, but not to expiate his own guilt. The patient's reactions to the error should then be explored in terms of his own problems. Confessing shortcomings to a patient who feels negatively about the therapist undermines the therapeutic relationship. Dealing with patients' negative feelings through expressions of friendliness may heighten guilt, intensify anger, and increase the distance between therapist and patient. Patients' hostile feelings should be acknowledged neutrally if possible. They require physical restraint if they endanger therapist or patient.

On occasion, an overt emotional reaction by the therapist is appropriate to indicate that he is not impervious and that he does react as a person. There are some patients who demand an overt reaction, who will rage or sulk until they have provoked one. However, studies of encounter groups suggest that display of the leader's contempt, dislike, and hostility in a nonaccepting emotional climate is damaging.[3]

There are only a few absolute indications for self-disclosure by the therapist: (1) when necessary to preserve the life of the patient or the therapist; (2) when some real event in the life of the therapist significantly alters the therapeutic relationship; and (3) when some aspect of the therapist as a person is severely disruptive of therapy.

The therapist must refrain from self-disclosure under certain circumstances. When a therapist's feelings about a patient, if expressed, would make it difficult for the patient to maintain his self-esteem, the therapist had best keep them to himself. If the therapist actively dislikes a patient, he should refrain from verbalizing it. If adequate exploration of the patient and therapist-related variables does not alter the therapist's feeling in a more positive direction, the therapist should arrange to transfer the patient to a therapist who can feel positively about him. The therapist should not make a pretense of liking a patient.

The therapist can acknowledge to himself but should refrain from acting on his omnipotent fantasies. It is belittling to feel that one can only be rescued by the intervention of one's therapist, even though certain patients wish to be rescued by an all-powerful person. Furthermore, the therapist should not compete with the patient to see who is the more potent; he should not, for example, reassure a patient that he will *personally* keep the patient from running away or from doing harm to himself or others.

What Are Appropriate Object-Need Gratifications between Therapist and Patient?

The therapist needs to gratify his patient's object needs sufficiently to maintain the treatment relationship, but not to the extent that he undermines the patient's relationships with other important people in his life. A therapeutic relationship is not a substitute for a family or a social life. The therapist, on the other hand, must allow himself sufficient gratification in the relationship that he can work with the patient, while taking care that such gratification does not stalemate the treatment, eclipse his life away from the office, or, by virtue of its importance to him, undermine his professional judgment.

The therapist has several courses of action available should his relationship with the patient become damaging to either one. He begins by examining his reactions to the patient, asking himself what is countertransference and what is based on current happenings within himself, in his outside life, or between himself and the patient. Intense chaotic feelings in the therapist may be one of the first clues that he is working with a borderline patient. If the difficulties persist, he can turn to the patient for the latter's assessment of the situation. If there is still no satisfactory outcome, the therapist can seek consultation, supervision, or treatment for himself. And of course, the patient has the option of seeking another opinion or another therapist.

Psychotherapy is a highly complex undertaking and a difficult way to earn a living. Every therapist is vulnerable, and there are certain times when he is more vulnerable than others. Therapists, as are all human beings, are inevitably frustrated in their daily lives. They experience the death of loved ones, growing apart from spouses, growing up of children, and failure to reach cherished (but irrational) goals. Each frustration or disappointment stimulates the urge to turn to one's patients for comfort and acceptance. It is easy for the therapist to fantasize that certain of his patients would never leave him, others would always admire him, and still others would make sacrifices to be with him. At these times, the therapist must be aware of the burden he is tempted to place on his patients and consider if it is in their mutual best interest. Occasionally, a patient's self esteem is enhanced by the therapist's willingness to lean on him temporarily during a crisis in the therapist's life.

The tendency to exploit patients for one's own needs may be subtle. Because of the subtleties involved, every therapist must periodically turn to his colleagues to help maintain his balance in the stream of unconscious forces in his own life and the lives of his patients.

Concluding Remarks

In conclusion, I find no innate curative power in self-disclosure. Its power is determined by the same factors that affect the potency of any therapeutic activity: its dosage, timing (or context), and content. The concepts of dosage, timing, and content derive from the medical model of psychotherapy, in which a lay person turns to a professional for expert guidance. Caring for a patient as a person and demonstrating that caring is simply not enough. The motivation to be psychologically helpful in the absence of an awareness of psychopathology and psychodynamics is no more effective in the treatment of emotional disorders than is the motivation to relieve the symptoms of appendicitis without an awareness of anatomy and physiology. There are few people who are innately psychologically helpful to such a degree that they never do damage. Most mental health professionals are ordinary, well-motivated people who require training and discipline to become useful as helpers. The ordinary psychotherapist requires guidelines. These guidelines are not absolute limits but rather a frame of reference and checklist that enable the professional helper to approach the bewildering complexity of another human being in a coherent manner. This frame of reference may not provide the answer to each patient's problems, but it does provide a basic structure that therapist and patient alike can use as they jointly attempt to construct an approach to the patient's life situation.

References

1. Truax, C. D., and Mitchell, K. M.: Research in certain therapist interpersonal skills in relation to process and outcome. In *Handbook of Psychotherapy and Behavior Change.* A. E. Bergen and S. L. Garfield, eds. John Wiley, New York, 1971.

2. Searles, H. F.: *Collected Papers on Schizophrenia and Related Subjects.* International Universities Press, New York, 1965, p. 653.

3. Lieberman, M. A., Yalom, I. D. and Miles, M. B.: *Encounter Groups: First Facts.* Basic Books, New York, 1973.

Index

Chessick, R. D., 122, 124
Chester, P., 94
Cody, Frank, 40
Communicative matching, 118
Confrontation, role in therapy, 65–66
Congruence, defined, 16
Cooperation, role in therapy, 48
Cotherapists: advantages, 142–143; disadvantages, 143–144; in group therapy, 142–148; ideal interaction, 145; identification of patient with, 5; male-female, 143; married, 148; marital counseling by, 32; relation between, 5, 32; self-disclosure by, 146–147
Counteridentification, 125
Countertransference: with borderline, 124; clues to identification of, 47, 154, 158–159; defined, 47, 152–153; and therapist disclosure, 61, 152–159

Dahlberg, C. C., 94
Defense mechanisms: borderline, 116; psychotherapeutic views of, 11, 14, 15
Deprivation, role in therapy, 54–55
Disclosingness, nonpatient, studies of, 36–37. See also Self, use of; Therapist disclosure
Drag, L. R., 36
Dynamic level of intervention, 62

Ego splitting, defined, 118
Ego structure: adolescent, 108–109; borderline, 116, 118–120; in group therapy, 136–137; relation to disclosure, 56–57, 81–82
Ego-supportive therapy, 51–53; for adolescent, 106; for borderline, 116; group, 131–133, 136–137; patient's feelings toward therapist in, 59; use of self-disclosure in, 74–75, 168
Empathy: and symbiotic transference, 97–98; therapist's use of, 64
Encounter groups: failure, 133; research, 37–39
Evocative therapies, 53–58; for adolescents, 106; group, 133–135; patient's feelings toward therapist in, 59; use of self-disclosure in, 75–78, 168
Existential therapy, 3–4; technical processes of, 14; view of empathy, 64; view of self-disclosure, 14–15
Exploration, as mode of intervention, 66

Facilitation, as mode of intervention, 65–66
Family therapy, for adolescents, 107
Fantasy: adolescent, 109; therapist, 28–29
Feedback: in ego-supportive therapies, 74–75; in group therapies, 132–133
Feelings: borderline, 116–117; here and now, 40, 124–125; disclosure of, 25–27, 40, 85–86, 112. See under Patient; Therapist
Ferenczi, Sandor, 12–13
Formulations, definition, 28

Freud, Anna, 52
Freud, Sigmund, 11–13, 76–77, 136

Genetic level of intervention, 62
Genuineness, defined, 15
Gestalt therapy, 133, 134
Greenson, R. R., 14, 74–75, 96
Group therapist, 133–135; problems, 130
Group therapies: advantages, 128; coleadership, 142–148; ego strength in, 136–137; elements of, 132; relationships in, 31–32; resistances in, 140. *See also* Encounter groups; Marathon group therapies

Havens, L. L., 125
Here-and-now feelings, 40, 62, 124–125
Hill, L. B., 82
Honesty, 89–91, 96
Humanistic psychology, 10; view of self-disclosure, 15–16
Humor, role in therapy, 78, 91–92
Hurley, J. R., 37
Hurley, S. J., 37

Identification: defensive, 144; in ego-supportive therapies, 75; in group therapies, 133; projective, 118–119, 123; role in therapy, 5, 48, 52–53, 163. *See also* Modeling theory
Idealization: borderline, 123; primitive, 18
Insight: intellectual versus emotional, 49; use in therapy, 5, 48

Interpretation, use in therapy, 28, 66

Jourard, S. M., 15, 36, 37
Jourard Self-Disclosure Questionnaire, 37
Journey into Self (Carl Rogers), 16

Kangas, J. A., 42
Keeping looking, existential, 4
Kernberg, O., 115, 118, 120, 124
Kohut, H., 122
Korntreich, M., 44
Kubie, L. S., 78, 91

Langs, R. J., 153
Leader: in group therapy, 136; qualities of, 38–39
Learning, role in therapy, 48
LeBon, G., 136
Levy, Jacques, 17–18
Lewis, J. M., 145
Lieberman, M. A., 37, 89–90, 133

McCartney, J. L., 100–101
McDanald, E. C., 83, 98–99, 117–118
Malan, D. H., 129
Malone, T. P., 14–15
Marathon group therapy, 17–18, 28, 133–134
Marital counseling, 32
Masterson, J. F., 118, 125
May, Rollo, 10
Meltzhoff, J., 44
Menninger, K., 13
Miles, M. B., 37

Mintz, E. E., 17, 85, 134
Modeling theory, 16–17

Nadelson, T., 125
Neutrality, 9–18, 166

Objectification, 9
Object needs: 59, 61, 170–171. *See also* Physical contact; Sexual intimacy
Otstott, R. I., 42

Patient: adolescent versus adult, 105; demand for openness by, 25; disclosure, relation to therapist disclosure, 40–44; effect of cotherapy on, 146, 147–148; effect of physical contact on, 98–99; effect of therapist disclosure on, 2–5; ego strength, 56–57; feelings toward therapist, 58–59, 83–84, 92–93, 123, 139–140; object needs, 59, 99–101, 170–171; reaction to therapist error, 158. *See also* Adolescent patient; Borderline patient
Patient-therapist relationship, 82–83; guidelines, 5–6; and honesty, 167; object need gratification in, 170–171; and self disclosures, 80
Patient-therapist relationship, real (nontransference), 55–56, 78–81; for adolescent, 106–107; for borderline, 120–122; in groups, 135–136
Perls, F. H. (Fritz), 95–96
Personality: adolescent, 106;

borderline, 115, 117; therapist, 153. *See also* Ego structure
Physical contact, 113, 118, 124, 141; impact, 29–30; problems, 98–101. *See also* Sexual intimacy
·Powell, W. J., 36
Premature closure, 4
Projection, 119
Psychoanalysis, view of self-disclosure, 11–14
Psychodrama, 133, 134

Rachman, A. W., 17
Reality testing: adolescent, 108–109; borderline, 115, 117; improved by disclosure, 165
Recovery, Inc., 131
Regression, 104, 106, 117, 54
Reich, W., 100–101
Repressive therapies, 50–51; for adolescents, 106; group, 130–131, 136–137; patient's feelings about therapist in, 59, 83–84; self-disclosure in, 73–74, 168
Resistance, 96–97
Respect, role in therapy, 84–85, 164
Robertiello, R. C., 17, 85, 134–135
Rogerian psychotherapy, 2
Rogers, Carl, 10–11, 16, 25–26
Rosenfield, H. A., 13–14
Rosson, Barry, 40

Schizophrenics, 43–44, 166
Schmideberg, M., 117
Schwartz, E. K., 64
Scrutchins, M. P., 42
Searles, H. F., 98, 117, 166

Wexler, M., 76
Whitaker, C. A., 14–15
Whitehorn, J. C., 43, 64
Winnicott, D. W., 125
Wolf, A., 64

Wolf man (Sigmund Freud's), 11–12, 166

Yalom, I. D., 37, 131–132, 148